MW00635081

Rooted and Growing

A History of the Saint Paul Garden Club
1927–2013

Photo: Sally Ordway Irvine (Mrs. Thomas E.) at the
family summer place on Cedar Island in Wisconsin
about 1970

Rooted and Growing

A History of the Saint Paul Garden Club
1927–2013

Deni Svendsen, Historian
Marge Hols, Editor
Judy MacManus, Designer
Club Members, Authors

Saint Paul Garden Club
Founded 1927

© 2013 by Saint Paul Garden Club
Manufactured in the United States of America.
10 9 8 7 6 5 4 3 2 1
Library of Congress Control Number 2013908127
ISBN 978-0-578-13334-8

All rights reserved. No part of this publication
may be reproduced in any manner without prior written permission.
For inquiries or permissions, contact the publisher:
Saint Paul Garden Club
www.saintpaulgardenclub.org
Digital printing by Blurb

Front cover: Early members of the Saint Paul Garden Club
toured a member's garden in 1934; from left: Mrs. Edwin White,
Mrs. John G. Ordway, Mrs. C.O. Kalman, Mrs. John W. Daniels,
Mrs. Stanley Gates and Mrs. Horace Irvine. Back cover:
The garden of Charlotte Ordway (Mrs. John G.) on White Bear
Lake, Dellwood, in the late 1950s. Illustration credits:
All images are from Saint Paul Garden Club
archives except for images listed on Page 156,
which are published by permission.

Saint Paul Garden Club
Founded 1927
Member of The Garden Club of America since 1933

Contents

Preface

Four years ago the Saint Paul Garden Club was asked by the Garden Club of America to compile a history of our organization for the GCA Centennial in 2013. Our club decided to write a book containing articles about the founding members, past and present projects, and biographical sketches of members associated with some of the major projects.

What a delight it has been to rediscover and document the breadth and depth of our club's leadership in the community! Our members funded land to expand the fledgling Minnesota Landscape Arboretum in Chanhassen. They initiated enduring programs including the Children's Hospital Green Plant Therapy Program, Minnesota Green and Blooming Saint Paul. They cared for the Governor's Residence gardens for many years and, to this day, plant and maintain the gardens in Rice Park in downtown Saint Paul. They funded all manner of environmental restoration projects, as small as providing plants for an elementary school prairie in Mahtomedi and as large as transforming Swede Hollow into a Saint Paul nature park. It's with wonder and admiration that we preserve and share these stories and many more with the club and community.

Recording Shared Memories

A History Book Committee has worked on this project since July 2009. We began by holding a Reunion Tea for our sustaining members to record shared memories of their active years in the club. The daunting task of reorganizing the club archives was accomplished by the diligent work of two University of Minnesota interns working on their master's degrees in horticulture, Karine Pouliquen and Lori Schindler. We compiled the club's allocations and contributions to the community through the years from available records. We are grateful to Anne Ferrell and Ellie Bruner for preparing this valuable financial record.

More than 40 club members researched and wrote articles for the book. We encouraged new members to interview previous ones and find photographs. Our club is fortunate to have talented members with writing backgrounds who each wrote several articles. I especially want to thank Marge Hols and Judy MacManus. Marge, our editor, added professionalism and polish to our articles. Judy, club president in 2010-12 and a graphics designer, leant her considerable talents to designing this beautiful book.

As club historian, I wondered what we would gain from this project. Would the interviews reconnect previous, older members with newer ones? Yes, and new friendships were formed and an appreciation fostered for the wonderful accomplishments of these earlier garden club members. Would the membership sustain interest in this project over several years? Yes, authors presented their articles at our general meetings as an ongoing series on our club's history. Last year, the club held a flower show at the Minnesota History Center in Saint Paul with the theme, "The Way We Were," based on our club history.

We decided to tell our story by organizing the articles into categories reflecting our mission statement: The purpose of the Saint Paul Garden Club shall be:
1) To stimulate the joy of gardening and to promote horticultural knowledge;
2) To encourage the best in design, creation and development of public and private gardens;
3) To restore, improve and protect the environment through action in the field of conservation, civic plantings and educational programs; and
4) To share the advantages of association by means of meetings, conferences, correspondence and publications.

Contributing to Community

Would the club, started as a social group by some prominent ladies with a common interest in gardening, be judged as relevant today? The founders were from families that valued volunteerism. Has our club continued its legacy of contributing to the community? Compiling this garden club history has helped assure us that our club has become even more relevant today because of our growth into the wider community.

The club has supported projects addressing the changing climate and other pressing environmental needs. We have contributed our efforts and grants to beautify public spaces in Saint Paul and surrounding communities. We have delighted and educated the public with our flower shows and contributed financially to educational programs. We have continued the legacy of our founders with our volunteer work and honored the traditions of "old Saint Paul" by continuing the Holiday Tea Dance as our family gathering and fund-raising event. Also, by compiling this history, we have celebrated the accomplishments of our past, which, in turn, encourage us to face the challenges and chart the directions for our future.

Deni Svendsen, Historian

Rooted and Growing
Garden Club Founders

The seeds were sown in 1927, during the light-hearted lull between the two world wars, when a group of 32 friends with a passion for gardens gathered to form a club. Whether they met at a home in Crocus Hill, on Summit Avenue, or in one of their summer cottages on White Bear Lake, we don't know. But to this day, a favored spot for a monthly meeting of the Saint Paul Garden Club is at a member's home.

Our founders were ladies who managed their households, staff and gardens. They conscientiously volunteered within the community and exercised their newly acquired right to vote. Meetings offered members and guests a chance to enjoy the gardens of the hostess before getting down to business. A program was followed by tea. After Prohibition was lifted in 1933 something stronger might have been offered as well. My sister, Polly Olmstead, remembers such an occasion fifty years ago at the lovely summer home of Charlotte Ordway, who was known to us as "Auntie Ta." After members viewed a demonstration of the proper way to divide iris, a waiter came around with frozen daiquiris on a silver tray.

Joined Garden Club of America

The members' interest in conservation, floral design and horticulture weathered the dark cloud of the Great Depression. In 1933, the fledgling Saint Paul Garden Club was the one hundredth accepted into the Garden Club of America. With its new affiliation the garden club flourished. Founders invited friends and family to join. Jim Gardner remembers that his mother, Roberta (Mrs. Truman P.), was thrilled when she received an invitation in 1952 because it meant both her gardens and her knowledge of botanical plant names had passed inspection.

Today, our bylaws allow 130 members and we no longer keep records with only the members' married names, as was the case years ago. It took a bit of sleuthing, for example, to discover that Mrs. Horace Klein was Grace Trask Klein (Horace). As times have changed, so has our membership, which now includes many professional women, including garden writers and garden designers. Elisabeth Moles Ljungkull (Mrs. Rolf G.) was our very first Master Gardener. She is now in

Photo: Original garden club logotype

good company as several members enjoy that distinction. Today, many of us have help in the garden, as the founding ladies did, while others take pride in doing it all on their own.

Generations of Gardeners

Over the years, new generations of gardeners related to the founders by birth or marriage have joined our club. These second- and third-generation members have helped sustain the club, making great contributions as well as encouraging us to value our institutional history.

with plant allergies, but Alex makes her contribution by hosting flower show judges. Another granddaughter-in-law of Gladys is Catherine Nicholson.

Diane Roth and her talented daughter, Sally Brown, both current members, remember Great Aunt Helen Schutte Kueffner, another founder.

Nancy Weyerhaeuser's mother-in law, Peggy Weyerhaeuser Harmon, was a member whose mother-in-law was founder Harriette Davis Weyerhaeuser. Through her late husband, W. John, Lee Driscoll is also related to this founder.

Marla Ordway is the daughter-in-law of Marge Ordway, who passed in 2013. Marge's mother-in-law was founder Charlotte Partridge Ordway.

Twinks Irvine and Deb Irvine are current members who married descendents of Sally Ordway Irvine and Thomas Irvine. This makes them in-laws of two founders, Charlotte Partridge Ordway and Clotilde McCullough Irvine.

Susan Cross is the daughter of a member, Arline Griggs Mills, and granddaughter of a founder, Arline Bayliss Griggs. Ethel Griggs is also connected to this founder.

Through her husband's family,

Among current members, Susan McCarthy and her sister, Priscilla Brewster, are third-generation members. Susan's mother-in-law, Alex Bjorkland, is the daughter of founder Gladys Ford Ordway. Alex laughs because her mother had two daughters

Photo: A 1935 garden club gathering. Seated, from left: Mrs. H.T. Drake, Mrs. Stanley Gates, Mrs. A.H. Harmon, Mrs. John W. Daniels, Mrs. Archibald MacLaren. Standing: Mrs. John S. Abbott, Mrs. W.R. Kueffner, Mrs. M.W. Griggs, Mrs. Edwin White, Mrs. Albert Schuneman, Mrs. Thomas L. Daniels, Mrs. C.O. Kalman, Mrs. F.E.B. Foley, Mrs. E.B. Ober.

Tottie Lilly is related to founder Rachel Cunningham Lilly.

Pegi Jaffray Harkness is the great niece of founder Geraldine Schurmeier Thompson, and the niece of Charlotte Hannaford Drake, who passed in 2006.

Clover Fobes Earl, who passed in 2008, was the granddaughter of founder Clotilde McCullough Irvine and the niece of Clotilde's daughter, Olivia Irvine Dodge.

We're all grateful to the founders of the Saint Paul Garden Club, happy to be affiliated with the Garden Club of America and proud of our contributions to the community over the years. We'd like to think that our founders would be pleased to see the results of their vision in 1927.

Susan Cross

Saint Paul Garden Club Founders 1927

Linda Baker Ames (Mrs. Charles Lesley)
Glenn Bend (Mrs. Harold P.)
Markell Conley Brooks (Mrs. Edward)
Amelia Leonard Daniels (Mrs. John W.)
Frances Mertens Daniels (Mrs. Thomas L.)
Emma B. Drake (Mrs. H.T.)
Jean Foley (Mrs. Edward)
Elizabeth Dearth Foley (Mrs. Frederick E.B.)
Kathleen Thompson Gates (Mrs. Stanley)
Arline Bayliss Griggs (Mrs. Milton Wright)
Eleanor Hammond (Mrs. J. Felton)
Clotilde McCullough Irvine (Mrs. Horace Hills)
Alexandra Kalman (Mrs. C. Oscar)
Clara Cook Kellogg (Mrs. Frank B.)
Grace Trask Klein (Mrs. Horace)
Helen Schutte Kueffner (Mrs. William)
Carrie Drake Lightner (Mrs. William Hurley)
Rachel Cunningham Lilly (Mrs. Richard C.)
Katherine Dean MacLaren (Mrs. Archibald)
Charlotte Partridge Ordway (Mrs. John Gilman)
Jessie Gilman Ordway (Mrs. Lucius Pond)
Gladys Ford Ordway (Mrs. Richard)
Katherine Gillette Prampoline (Mrs. Alberto)
Virginia Schuneman Richards (Mrs. E.T. Fraser)
Mary Proal Saunders (Mrs. Edward Nelson, Jr.)
Louise Nelson Schuneman (Mrs. Albert Lesley)
Gretchen Richter Stott (Mrs. Charles W.)
Dorothy Thompson
Geraldine Schurmeier Thompson (Mrs. Horace)
Harriette Davis Weyerhaeuser (Mrs. F.E.)
Anne Turney White (Mrs. Edwin)
Margaret Ames Wright (Mrs. Cushing F.)

Photo, from left: Mrs. Roger Shepard, Mrs. Charles Leslie Ames, garden club president, and Mrs. J. Felton Hammond in spring, 1928

Charlotte Ordway, Mover and Shaper

A note from our garden club archive: "Charlotte (Mrs. John G.) Ordway has done more to shape the Garden Club of Saint Paul than any other member. It was she who was president when we were accepted for membership in the Garden Club of America in 1933. She served on the Board of Directors of the GCA from 1940 to 1943 and was Zone Chairman from 1948 to 1950.

Her enthusiasm was stimulating and contagious, and her garden was an inspiration to all. She loved the garden club and wanted it to achieve prestige and recognition nationally. To this end, she worked unceasingly, locally as well as nationally. She lobbied, arranged flowers, chaired committees, solicited funds—no job was too demanding or too menial. She set an example for all to follow. In 1968 Mrs. Ordway became an honorary member of our club."

Photo, top: Charlotte Ordway (Mrs. John G.); bottom: Mrs. Ordway's formal rose garden in 1962

Photo: Preparing for the garden club's 1932 Tulip Show were Eleanor Hammond (Mrs. J. Felton) and Charlotte Ordway (Mrs. John G.).

*Stimulate the Joy of Gardening
and Promote Horticultural Knowledge*

Flower Shows
Showcasing Our Creativity

Flower shows have been a long-standing tradition for garden clubs and the Saint Paul Garden Club is no exception. The fledgling club held its first Mid-Summer Flower Show in July, 1929, at the White Bear Yacht Club. Specimen Blooms, Flower Arrangement and Luncheon Table for Six were among six classes in the Show Schedule. "Our flower exhibits…were perfectly splendid and augur very well what heights we shall reach in future years," wrote Linda Ames (Mrs. C. Lesley), the club's first president.

The following summer, Miss Helen Bunn hosted a club flower show at her home on Manitou Island, White Bear Lake. Harriette Weyerhaeuser (Mrs. F.E.) won first place for an arrangement of garden flowers and Geraldine Thompson (Mrs. Horace) won for her pink peonies. In June, 1931, Miss Bunn's home was also the

scene of the club's Peony Show.

In 1932, members expanded the Mid-Summer Show at the yacht club to eight classes, including a Miniature Garden, Flower Arrangement for a hall table and a Breakfast Tray. The show was judged and ribbons were awarded. Show admission was 50 cents; proceeds were used for improvements in Saint Paul parks. In the later 1930s, and

resuming after World War II in the late 1940s, club flower shows were held at the University Club in Saint Paul.

From 1956 through the late 1970s, the club's flower shows were one-day affairs held in private homes, often during the annual meeting. In June, 1961, the flower show was chaired by Marion Fry (Mrs. Robert) and Ruth Shepard (Mrs. S.M., Jr.) and held

Photo: Club horticulture exhibits at Eastcliff mansion, Saint Paul, 2004 at the home of Frannie Budd (Mrs. John). Club members were urged to enter at least two floral arrangement classes and were allowed up to two specimens in each horticulture class. To quote from the chairman's report, "Mrs. Budd will serve coffee and dessert, and kindly bring your own sandwich."

Miniature Arrangements

In 1966, the first mention of a Miniatures Class appeared: "Miniature arrangement using furniture and flowers arranged in a three-sided lady's shoe box with an open top." The show was held at the home of Jane Ridder (Mrs. B.H., Jr.) in Sunfish Lake and lunch was again served. Flower shows continued to be one-day affairs and were held each year until 1990. In the 1985 report, "Blooming Masterpieces," we see the first mention of community service in regard to a flower show. "Six nursing homes were invited, at half-hour intervals during the afternoon, to view the show and have cookies and juice." Although only four nursing homes participated, the residents' enthusiasm was noted. The report also noted Mother Nature's capriciousness: "Don't hold the show three days after a hail storm or after five days of cold and gray weather." Apparently there were challenges that year.

Following a tradition of working together, the Saint Paul Garden Club and Lake Minnetonka Garden Club held their first joint flower show in 1987 at the Guthrie Theater. The theme, appropriately, was "Stages of Summer." After that, the garden club decided that a flower show was just too much work for one day.

Botanical Names Required

The 1989 flower show, "Perception of Bloom," marked the Garden Club of America's initiation of a new requirement: All plant material must be labeled with botanical and common names. It's a requirement that continues to befuddle club members: What *is* the genus of that plant?

Our horticulture stars were Elisabeth Ljungkull (Mrs. Rolf G.) and Charlotte Drake (Mrs. Carl B., Jr.). Engraved silver award trays show Elisabeth winning the Shepard Horticulture Award and the

Photos, from left: Miniature arrangements; and Harriette Weyerhaeuser (Mrs F. E.) and Eleanor Hammond (Mrs. J. Felton) with a mass arrangement, 1934

Horticulture Lilies Award at seven of eight shows in the 1980s. Charlotte followed with five horticulture and lily awards at consecutive shows in the 1990s.

Flower shows continued to be held every one to two years through the 1990s. In 1997, Lucy Fellows, author

of our garden club newsletter, provided the following description for "The Summer Reading List." "The show was large and lavish and hordes of judges descended on Saint Paul. Clover Earl was the big winner in flower arranging,

and, in the vegetable category, a ten-pound radish brought squeals of delight."

The 1997 show was the club's first GCA Small Flower Show, organized according to GCA requirements. Clover Earl and Vicky Holman spent more than a year putting the show together. "That was the beginning of our club becoming a legitimate small flower show location, complete with national GCA judges," Vicky said. "We had five classes in the show; judges helped us assess whether the classes we proposed met the standards. Before then, we had only inter-club flower shows."

Our shows, held every three years, are public affairs held in large venues including the Science Museum of Minnesota, Marjorie McNeely Conservatory at Como Park and, in 2012, the Minnesota History Center. Each show is a major undertaking,

including a preview party and two days of public viewing. Club members work hard planning and setting up

the show. GCA judges are brought in from around the country and there is serious competition for the prestigious national awards. The real highlight of each show, however, remains the delight in seeing all the entries and "oohing and aahing" over them.

Bonnie Hollibush and Judy MacManus

18

A Profile

Marge Ordway, Continuing a Family Legacy

Marge Ordway (Mrs. J.G., Jr.) had been a member of the Saint Paul Garden Club longer than any other current member, 55 years, when she passed away in January 2013. In 2002 she was made an Honorary Member. Marge held membership in two other Garden Club of America (GCA) clubs: Jupiter Island, her home in Florida where she had been very active, and Lake Minnetonka, where she spent her summers.

Born a "Minneapolis girl," Marge summered with her family on White Bear Lake. It was there she met her future spouse at White Bear Yacht Club dances. While attending Finch College in Manhattan she reconnected with John, son of Charlotte Partridge Ordway, on the steps of the Yale Club. The couple scheduled their wedding for June 28, 1947. Her future mother-in-law, president of our garden club, was heavily involved in the GCA Annual Meeting scheduled in Saint Paul June 24–27, 1947, but Marge was totally unaware of that. Charlotte, very polite and proper, never let on that this date was inconvenient. She prepared for both events, housing guests and attending everything. "After I grew up, so to speak, and joined the garden club I felt so badly," Marge said. "I didn't realize the kind of thing it was."

In 1954, Marge was put up for membership in the garden club, where her mother-in-law and many family members, including Gladys Ordway and Sally Irvine, already belonged. She was living in the old "Archer House" at 26 Dellwood Avenue. Back then, a garden club member made a surprise white-glove inspection tour of each candidate's garden. Agnes Ober dropped in on Marge as her family arrived home from a weekend house party in Northern Wisconsin. Marge described her gardens as "…a mess, all weeds." The family had moved in only recently and the gardens were not developed to her standards. The gardens passed, however, and Marge was admitted to the club. "I think she was afraid to turn me down because of Charlotte," Marge said.

Photo: Marge Ordway (Mrs. John G., Jr.)

Floral Designer and Judge

Marge became a wonderful floral designer and, in 1989, a GCA Judge; later, she was a Judge Emeritus. "Judging can be nerve wracking," she recalled. "I remember in South Carolina going around with two old ladies who were so tough. I may have been a provisional and they were very intimidating." Nevertheless she traveled the country to judge flower arranging, as it was then called, and researched the theme of every show.

In 2000, Marge received the GCA Club Flower Arrangement Certificate. She will be remembered for many Best in Show awards, especially in "The Times of Our Lives" show at the Town and Country Club in Saint Paul. Her entry was a foyer piece for a foreign students' going-away party. The Norwegian scene featured mirror pieces shaped like mountains, lots of small evergreens and silica gel resembling a stream. Many of us still remember it. Table classes were also a favorite of hers and she was very successful in entering them. In a Jupiter Island show there was a shortage of entries in the Renaissance Era Table Class. Marge and a friend convinced their spouses to enter and provided all the materials. "The boys" were excited to take Third Place.

Several of GCA Zone XI's current members credit Marge with being their inspiration as floral designers. Gay Estes, a revered GCA judge herself, shared her thoughts: "… Marge had a quiet dignity and was meticulous. She was highly regarded…. I did judge with her a few times and she was wonderful. She was a lovely dresser and quite handsome."

Marge was president of the Saint Paul Garden Club in 1973-75. "I went to five GCA Annual Meetings in wonderful places. I don't know why I was able to go when I was so young," she said. Marge also served on the GCA Admissions Committee with her friend Nan Field; they continued their friendship in Florida. Her friends from GCA and memories of these Annual Meetings were very special to her.

When the Minnesota Landscape Arboretum expanded, Charlotte Ordway led our garden club to fund the land purchase. Marge followed in her footsteps, championing

Photo: Marge Ordway demonstrated a floral design at Pam Attia's home.

fundraising for the arboretum and serving as a trustee. Her love of beauty also led her to serve on the boards of the Minneapolis Institute of Arts and Guthrie Theater, as did many of her garden club friends.

In the 1980s, the Ordway family provided significant funds to the Japanese Garden at Como Zoo and Conservatory. The garden was named in Charlotte Ordway's honor. A few years later Marge and Smokey (John) contributed a Japanese Garden to the Minnesota Landscape Arboretum.

Morning Meetings 'Unladylike'

Garden club meetings used to start at 2 p.m. "Nine a.m. meetings like we have now would have been considered unladylike," Marge said. "We had our meeting and our speaker and then we had tea. Everyone had a tea service and there would be one at both ends of the table. You would be asked to pour. Meetings were bigger in the summertime."

Marge's most memorable garden club event was mentioned by other senior members so it must have been quite the affair. "Jane Ridder had a morning meeting at her home in Sunfish Lake around her pool," Marge recalled. "There was also a floral arrangement sale in her barn. She served a very potent gin cocktail before lunch and the very dignified old gals (they were probably in their fifties) had way too many. Lunch was delayed while they drank. Jane was very worried how she was going to get them out of there. They were heavy drinkers back then."

Marge's words of advice for the future of the garden club? "Keep the city of Saint Paul in mind. Work to beautify Saint Paul."

Marla Ordway and Deni Svendsen

Photo: Marge Ordway served tea at a garden club meeting.

The Art of Flower Arranging

The art and love of flower arranging stands out as one of the core tenets of the Saint Paul Garden Club. From the very beginning, flower arrangements were provided for meetings and luncheons by the event hostesses.

"Flower arranging workshops originated in going to people's homes," Vicky Holman recalled. "They would often have an arrangement done for each room in the home." In the garden club's June 1993 newsletter, Lucy Fellows highlighted an upcoming workshop: "You may hone your arranging skills at Vicky Holmen's. She is generously offering two workshops featuring Period Arrangements at her new house at 2543 Manitou Island."

Back in the 1940s, garden club members delivered flowers to the veterans at the Minnesota veterans' homes. One of our members recalled a veteran who broke down in tears at the sight of a rose bouquet. It had been

years since he had seen and smelled a fresh, garden-cut rose.

Since our garden club annual tea dances began in 1980, flower arrangements have been a central element of the event's design and ambiance. Each year there is great camaraderie among members in assembling the arrangements and then purchasing them for use in their

own homes over the holiday season. Recently, some members have chosen to donate their arrangements to nursing home residents and elderly former members.

In recent years, some of our members have showcased arrangements at the Minneapolis Institute of Arts' annual Art in Bloom event. For her design, each entrant

Photo, from left: Ellen Fridinger, Lou Schatz, Sarah Meek, Emily Gatto and Christine Umhoefer attended a floral design workshop at Koehler & Dramm.

takes inspiration from a work of art and the arrangement is displayed beside it.

Transition to Modern Designs

Garden club members were at the forefront of the transition from the traditional mass arrangement styles to modern, structural designs. For example, the design focus of Lucy Fellows was the English mass arrangement with lots of color—complemented by her personal trademark of dressing like a "million dollars" in Chanel style. Lucy, club president in 1988-89 and a member from 1979 to 2009, put on flower arranging demonstrations for club members. Her colorful arrangements, wardrobe and style also came to life in the club newsletters she joyfully penned for many years.

Our pioneers of contemporary ikebana design were Clover Earl and Vicky Holman. They used many unusual, nontraditional containers as the starting point of an arrangement. Clover, a member from 1970 to 2008, sponsored Vicky when she joined the club in 1976.

Although Clover's initial focus was horticulture, Vicky influenced

Clover to get involved in flower arranging. Their friendship grew as they collaborated on arrangements and entered Garden Club of America (GCA) flower shows around the country. Both won Certificates of Excellence at a Chicago flower show.

"For her contemporary designs Clover could take anything from around the house—a coffee pot, basket, wreath—and create an arrangement," Vicky recalled. "Her husband, George Earl, made containers for her. Clover became the trend-setter, both locally and nationally, in the style evolution from mass arrangement to the contemporary stylized look." Clover was a GCA flower arranging judge and secretary for the GCA's flower arranging magazine. "She was beautiful, giving, hard-working and probably held about every job in our club," Vicky said. She served as club president in 1985-86.

Miniatures Make the Scene

Betty Cammack and Lee Driscoll were early advocates of miniature arrangements, and Carol Kolb and Jean Rowland also became devotees, Barbie Braman Bentson recalled. But it wasn't until the mid-1990s, she said, that miniatures became an established class in flower shows. Barbie held an all-day

Photo: Vicky Holman with her floral arrangement in 1987

workshop at her home in about 2000 where members made miniature arrangements and critiqued them. In 2004, Barbie was one of only eight miniaturists nationally invited to exhibit at the prestigious Philadelphia Flower Show. "Let's Visit the American Wing" was the title of her exquisite miniature setting, which featured replicas of famous early American paintings and furniture garnished with unbelievably tiny green plants.

"The key is creativity," Barbie said. "It's really interesting to see how these things come about. Lee Driscoll does it in the most simple way and it's always just right. Nancy Hilger organized

members to create miniatures for the children's tables at one of our tea dances. Each enchanting creation was housed in a gallon mayonnaise jar. Sally Brown's miniatures are wonderful. Sally and Lucy Gehan won first place at our 2009 flower show with a darling little bear made out of ceramics with flowers all around it."

The art of flower arranging culminates in the flower show. No matter how big or small the show, the designer's challenge is to create an arrangement that interprets the class definition with creativity, beauty and style. Our members have run the

gamut of flower show participation, from intra-club flower shows through the major flower shows sponsored through the GCA. With many award winners and spectacular arrangements, these experiences provide treasured

memories, preserved in photos and recognition awards.

And, we can't think about flower arranging, without thinking about friendships: the camaraderie, the teamwork, and the beauty and joy in the outcome.

Sarah Meek, Marilee Elsholtz, Emily Gatto

Photos, from left: Barbie Braman and Lucy Fellows; Pam Nuffort with her floral hat; Nancy Hilger at Koehler & Dramm floral workshop

A Profile

Martha Ann Foote, Extraordinary Flower Arranger

Martha Ann Foote was nicknamed "Hank" by her husband, Jack, when he met her. When they married and came to live in Saint Paul, he introduced her to everyone by saying, "This is my wife, "Hank." Hank stuck. She preferred that people call her Martha, but agreed with her friend Joan Gardner that one would also have to indicate Hank somewhere.

Martha joined the Saint Paul Garden Club in 1967. She said it took awhile because she came here from out of town and didn't know anyone. She was living and working in Washington, D.C., when she met Jack. Martha grew up in Ohio and her family had a wonderful garden including Dorothy Perkins roses.

Jack dutifully took pictures of all Martha's prize-winning floral arrangements. Despite her many "firsts", he really wasn't all that impressed by the art form, Martha said. Joan and Vicky Holmen both remember her as an extraordinary arranger.

Flower-Arranging Lessons

Martha recalled that she and a carload of garden club members made weekly trips to Wayzata for flower-arranging lessons from Polly Chase, a Garden Club of America (GCA) judge. Polly was to be the key judge at the first flower show Joan chaired for the garden club. But, when Polly suffered a stroke three days before the show, her first conscious act was to ask her daughter-in-law to call Joan. Joan was told to call GCA headquarters, as GCA was obligated to supply another judge. As Joan remembers, the garden club was not even required to pay for transportation. Louise Benz offered her hospitality and put up the judge for her stay.

Martha's funniest memory was being assigned to hostess a GCA Zone XI meeting with Grace Beek on our club's behalf at the Minneapolis Institute of Arts. Under the influence of Madeline Murphy's

Photo: Martha Ann Foote (Mrs. Jack C.)

clothing culture (Madeline owned Frank Murphy's, an institution of ladies' fine clothing in Saint Paul), the two put on their best Ultrasuede suits and high heels. When they arrived at the art institute, everyone was wearing summer cotton print dresses and flat shoes. Martha said she and Grace laughed for the rest of their lives about their misery and embarrassment in having to run around all day in heels.

A garden club activity Martha remembered as special was a weekly commitment during the time she lived at Sunfish Lake. She and several other members delivered flower arrangements to the Veterans Administration Hospital. They painted or wrapped tin cans decoratively and filled them with flower arrangements from their gardens. Martha was still moved by the memory of the man who burst into tears upon receiving the flowers and said that he "…hadn't seen a rose in ten years."

Flower Show Hijinks

Martha recalled a garden club fund-raising activity at Jane Ridder's chicken coop. They had a flower show and a silent auction plus a spaghetti dinner. This was shortly before Joan joined the garden club, but she and her husband, Jim, were invited. The flower show included a men's flower-arranging class. Jack Foote had the florist at First Bank put together an arrangement for him. Martha objected strenuously, but Jack held his ground, saying this was all he knew about flower arranging. Jim Gardner found a rotten tire in his backyard and borrowed Joan's fish

pitcher, which was a ten-inch tall majolica knockoff. Jim put the pitcher in the center of the tire and filled it with grasses and water lilies. Meredith Alden, a friend of Joan's mother, rushed over to tell Joan that water lilies were on the protected list. Joan was mortified! The judges, already aware of the transgression, withdrew Jim's winning ribbon. Joan's happiest memory of this event was winning the bid on three sets of china, two different stacks of dessert plates and a set of dinner plates with Currier and Ives scenes.

When Joan interviewed Martha about the garden club's history in the summer of 2009, Martha was 99 years old. She passed away that November. She retained a clear memory and gracious manner until the end of her life. She and Jack served on many boards and in many volunteer positions, and were important contributing members of the Saint Paul community.

Joan Gardner

Minnesota State Horticultural Society

A Long-Term Collaboration

The Minnesota State Horticultural Society was founded in 1866 – one of the first in the nation. More than 60 years later the Saint Paul Garden Club was formed. By 1933, it had become an affiliated member of the horticultural society and since then the two have been stalwart partners.

During World War II, both organizations promoted victory gardens as a way to keep Americans well fed while our soldiers fought abroad to keep the world free. From 1941 to 1943, our club held study groups about victory gardens. The horticultural society magazine, then called *The Minnesota Horticulturist*, ran an article about victory gardens in a 1943 edition. Our club responded to its call and showed by the example of its members the difference that planting a vegetable garden in your back yard could make.

In 1988, the horticultural

society and garden club teamed up to champion the cause of "greening." Maureen Adelman was serving on the society board at the time. She remembers that our garden club invited the director of Philadelphia Green to speak to a large group of Twin Cities civic leaders about transforming "neighborhood eyesores" into local gardens. The idea caught

on here and Minnesota Green was organized. Model sites were launched in Minneapolis and Saint Paul and, in 1990, the program expanded statewide (see Minnesota Green).

From 2002 to 2012 five members served on the society's board of directors: Faye Duvall, Colles Larkin, Paula Soholt, Judy MacManus and Maureen Adelman, who served as

Photo: Resident gardeners, garden organizers and Master Gardeners celebrated the 2013 harvest of lush vegetables grown in Gardens-in-a-Box at the Sibley Manor Community Garden in Saint Paul.

board chair from 2009 through 2011. In 2011 and 2012, respectively, Maureen and Faye became the first members of our garden club to receive Life Awards from the horticultural society for their dedicated service.

For 18 years, the noted author and native-plant specialist Lynn Steiner served as editor-in-chief of the society's magazine, which changed its name to *Northern Gardener* while Lynn was at the helm. Lynn joined our garden club in 2012.

Our club has donated $27,550 to support projects of the horticultural society since 1957. Funds have been earmarked for many programs, including the society's fund to create the Minnesota Landscape Arboretum,

a building fund, general operations, a guest lecturer and vegetable garden awards. Since 2009, we have granted $12,000 to the society's innovative Garden-in-a-Box program. The program provides a raised garden structure, soil, vegetable plants and an information packet to low-income families and school children. The aim is to teach gardening and encourage healthy eating habits.

Bonnie Blodgett

Photos, from left: Honorees Maureen Adelman and Faye Duvall; Garden-in-a-Box

Minnesota Green

A Growing Idea

In 2013 there is widespread understanding that green spaces beautify neighborhoods, and that growing fresh food and flowers is good for our environment on multiple fronts. But 25 years ago this thinking was in its infancy. The Saint Paul Garden Club helped lead the way by inviting the director of Philadelphia Green to speak to a large group of Twin Cities' civic leaders about developing "neighborhood eyesores" into local gardens.

"It was Joanie Gardner's idea to invite J. Blaine Bonham, Jr., from Philadelphia Green to come to Saint Paul," said Colles Larkin, our conservation chair at that time. I called Mr. Bonham, and Rosalie Talen, conservation co-chair, and I arranged the meeting."

The idea caught the collective fancy of Mayor George Latimer and other leaders from Saint Paul's

city government and the state's Department of Trade and Economic Development, as well as the Minnesota State Horticultural Society. The concept was enthusiastically embraced by our garden club, with the horticultural society leading the initiative and funding. The result, today, is hundreds of community gardens across Minnesota cared for by

thousands of volunteers.

Minnesota Green launched in 1988 with model sites in Minneapolis and Saint Paul, and then expanded to service needs statewide by 1990. The model was based on partnerships in low- to moderate-income communities and neighborhoods. Services ranged from offering technical assistance in planning, land utilization and

Photo: Minnesota Green volunteers admired a garden in Riverside Park in 1991.

horticultural training to providing access to planting and construction materials. Minnesota Green became the link between resources and community needs. It coordinated resources of horticulture-related organizations, local and state governments and businesses to support community landscape improvements and encourage land stewardship.

On March 11, 1992, President Faye Duvall of our garden club received the American Community Gardening Award for outstanding contributions to Minnesota Green. Faye was a member of the initial steering committee that helped form Minnesota Green and later helped it develop into the only statewide community greening program in the nation at that time. Her leadership was a notable example of the vision and hands-on contributions from women of the garden club.

Minnesota Green continues to flourish as a program of the horticultural society, serving the greening efforts of thousands of volunteer gardeners throughout the state. It promotes community greening as a means to strengthen

neighborhoods through activities that connect people and plants, and is open to anyone interested in community gardening. One key service is a plant donation network for public spaces. Any group of gardeners involved in a community gardening project can sign up, pay a $55 annual fee, and

receive plants and supplies donated by growers, garden centers, nurseries and seed companies. Donations range from bare-root trees and shrubs to hardy perennials to thousands of flats of annuals. Minnesota Green also provides access to numerous community gardening networks and links, and sponsors a statewide awards program. Awards recognize individuals and organizations that have made outstanding contributions to greening efforts in public gardens and community projects.

Sarah Meek

Photo: A volunteer harvested eggplant in an award-winning garden on Columbus Ave. in South Minneapolis in 1991.

Green Plant Therapy
At Children's Hospitals and Clinics of Minnesota

The Green Plant Therapy Program at Children's–Saint Paul was initiated and sponsored by the Saint Paul Garden Club in 1989, and continues to this day. The project is well loved and supported by our members, and we have contributed operating grants totaling $32,675 since 1989.

The program was based in the hospital's fourth-floor greenhouse for many years. The greenhouse was a gift in 1983, four years after the hospital moved down the hill from Pleasant Avenue to its new home on Smith Avenue.

The basic idea behind the program is that while the hospital cares for them, the children care for a plant – something even more vulnerable than themselves. All children are invited to participate. They are encouraged to assemble pots, fill them, select plants from a cart after a brief horticulture lesson and pot their special plant. A

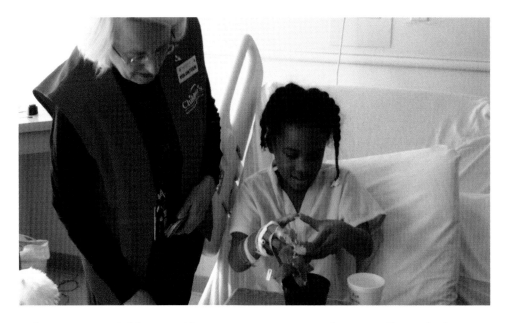

volunteer visits children unable to leave their rooms and pots a plant at their bedsides.

According to hospital staff, "Children gain mastery and self-esteem by potting and planting little green plants by themselves. It's an important source of relaxation therapy for very sick children."

"Children use tongue depressors, syringes without needles and other pieces of hospital equipment to plant seeds and mini-gardens," garden club member Joan Gardner reported in 1991. "They take their plants home with them and, occasionally, even return for a refill when a plant dies from over attention." Joan and Rosie Shepard were early club sponsors of the program.

Photo: An enthusiastic young patient planted a Christmas cactus with guidance from Nora Hornicek, a former Master Gardener.

Ramsey County Master Gardeners play a key role in this cooperative project. They volunteer to work with the children twice a week. Garden club member Sharon Prokosch volunteered when she was a Master Gardener.

Master Gardener Leonard Gloeb, (below) who manages the Green

Plant Therapy Program, has been volunteering at Children's Hospital for 25 years. He has devoted more than 13,500 hours to the program. Since the greenhouse was dismantled, he

houses all the plants at his home and transports them to the hospital.

Garden club archives show that plant therapy was not our first project with Children's Hospital. In 1927, our club's first year, members designed and planted a garden at the hospital's earlier site. In 1959 and 1960, crabapple trees and other plants were added.

In 2012, 27 garden club members individually contributed nearly $13,000 to sponsor an arbor on the hospital's new rooftop Storyland Garden. "Joan Gardner was the most instrumental person and a silent angel in this project," Catherine Nicholson

said. The garden, located off the pediatric intensive care unit, offers a refuge for children and their parents.

Cathy Colletti

Photos. from left: Joan Gardner (right) and her sister, Annie Harris; and fanciful arbors in the hospital's new rooftop Storyland Garden

Gibbs Museum
Preserving Our History

The Gibbs Museum of Pioneer and Dakotah Life is located in Falcon Heights between the busy urban centers of the Twin Cities on the 1849 farm of Heman and Jane Gibbs. The museum tells the true story of the interaction of two different cultures, the pioneers and the Dakota Indians, during the period of 1835-1862. The farm annually hosts 20,000 visitors and serves as a research and educational center for students.

The story of Gibbs Farm begins in 1835. Five-year-old Jane DeBow was taken by a missionary family traveling west to live among the Dakota Indian people near Fort Snelling and Lake Harriet in what is now Minneapolis. Playing with the Dakota children, Jane learned to speak their language and developed lifelong friendships with them.

In 1848, Jane married Heman Gibbs. Heman bought 160 acres in the

newly created Minnesota Territory in 1849, establishing Gibbs Farm. Using a trail from Lake Calhoun that crossed the farm on the way to wild rice lakes, the Dakotas would pitch their tipi and stay for weeks to visit their friend Jane. They were treated as honored guests at the farm. During this time, agricultural practices were taught to the Dakotas. Cloud Man was one of the first

Dakotas to accept these practices while maintaining the traditional migratory lifestyle.

Prairie-Flower Roof Planted

The relationship between the Saint Paul Garden Club and Gibbs Farm began in 1996 when the club granted $1,500 from its Community Fund for the historical landscaping of the original Gibbs farmhouse. In 1997,

Photo, from left: Charlotte Drake and Priscilla Brewster planted a wildflower roof on the dugout sod house at Gibbs Farm.

we provided $3,300 to restore the dugout sod house with a prairie-flower roof, which members helped install. A year later, the garden club gave $3,300 to plant a turtle-shaped Dakota Medicine Teaching Garden.

In 2001, our club received a Garden Club of America (GCA) Founders Fund finalist award of $5,000 for Gibbs Farm. Two of our members, Marla Ordway and Charlotte Drake, were also members of the Ramsey County Historical Society. Through their relationship with the society, our club chose Gibbs Farm as the project to nominate for the Founders Fund. Charlotte and Clover Earl worked with the society to define the project. Funds were used to provide handicapped accessibility to the original Dakota Indian Heritage Trail, and to create bilingual signs and programming to help urban Native Americans explore their heritage.

In 2005, our club gave $2,960 to Gibbs Farm to provide willow fencing and the services of Paul Red Elk, a native seed saver and cultural expert, to improve soil in the Dakota crop

garden. Descendants of Jane Gibbs and Cloud Man are active consultants to the farm.

Deb Venker

Photo: Yako Tahnaahga designed the turtle-shaped Dakota Medicine Teaching Garden.

Victory Gardens

A Teaching Moment

World War II brought changes for the Saint Paul Garden Club. The Garden Club of America delayed plans to hold its 1942 Annual Meeting in Saint Paul until after the war (1947). To save gasoline, our club voted to cut back to three planned meetings and the annual meeting, and directed its efforts to supporting the Victory Garden effort.

In 1943, members held study groups on victory gardens and taught how to rotate crops and interplant flowers and vegetables. In 1944, the club took an active part in the Saint Paul victory garden project of over 34,000 gardens. The club was awarded a certificate "in Grateful Recognition of Distinguished War Service in Cooperation with the USO" (United Service Organizations).

As early as 1942, the club had a speaker on victory gardens, Dr. L.E. Langley from the University of Minnesota Horticultural Science Department. Throughout 1943, club meetings included speakers on topics related to victory gardens. Daisy Abbott (Mrs. John S.) spoke on "Civic Victory Gardens" and Kathleen Gates (Mrs. Stanley) spoke on "Planning and Planting Our Own Victory Gardens." Edith Brooks (Mrs. Springer) used the amusing title, "Problems of a Vegetable Grower – or Worms in Our Private Lives." A related topic was "Problems and Methods of Canning." In September, at the home of Arline Griggs (Mrs. Milton W.), reports were given on victory gardens and storage of vegetables.

Karen Neset

Photo: Uncle Sam urged Americans to grow vegetables in World War I and II.

Camp Savage Garden
Helping the War Effort

During World War II, the Saint Paul Garden Club provided funds for a garden at Camp Savage, the site of a United States Military Intelligence Service Language School for Japanese-Americans. The school was located in Savage on 132 acres. The purpose of the school was to improve the Japanese language skills of Japanese-American soldiers so they could help translate documents, break codes and serve on the front lines in the Pacific Theater. The school was necessary because only seven percent of the Nisei – children of Japanese immigrants – were proficient in the Japanese language.

The garden club project, begun in May 1943, was spearheaded by Carolyn Lindeke (Mrs. Albert W.), who later served as garden club president in 1949-51. Club members worked at the camp throughout the summer, cleaning up, planting and landscaping. Plants were purchased

at a cost of $59.56. It is with pride the club can say it supported such a valuable part of the war effort.

The school was moved to Minnesota from San Francisco in 1942, after President Franklin D. Roosevelt's Executive Order 1066 in 1941 forced internment and relocation of Japanese-American families. A school with Nisei students on the West Coast was considered a national risk. Minnesota was chosen because of its excellent record of racial amity. Other midwestern states had been considered, but declined, and Gov. Harold Stassen agreed to take the school. The school was moved to Fort Snelling in 1944 after it outgrew Camp Savage.

Andrea McCue

Photo: Camp Savage, where our garden club helped create a garden in 1943.

Community Design Center

Garden Corps Youth Internships

On a beautiful late-summer morning in 2009, several members of the Saint Paul Garden Club toured one of seven gardens planted and maintained by young people in the Payne-Phalen community on Saint Paul's East Side. These fledgling gardeners were participating in the Garden Corps Youth Internship Program operated by the Community Design Center of Minnesota. The garden club has supported this program since 2002, granting funds totaling $19,350.

As we entered the garden's enclosed area, three high school girls greeted us warmly. Two were of Asian descent and one was American Indian. These girls had been responsible for planting and maintaining the garden throughout the summer months. The garden bloomed brightly with cosmos, bee balm, black-eyed Susan and sunflowers, which were interspersed between vegetables. The scent of herbs

tickled our noses.

As we walked through patches of peppers, broccoli, cabbages and corn, we could see that the organic and biodynamic gardening methods used by the garden corps yielded large, deeply colored and delectable looking vegetables. We also noted the many birds attracted by the colorful flowers and were told that the gardens were

designed to restore habitat for animals and migrating birds.

Our tour ended in a tomato patch where at least six different varieties were growing. We were invited to help ourselves to cherry tomatoes and didn't need a second invitation. As we munched on our yummy treat, the girls called our attention to four newly planted apple trees located just outside

Photo: Garden Youth Corps interns learned by doing in a community vegetable garden.

the garden, which were purchased partly with funds from our garden club.

The girls were anxious to share the notebook they had been keeping all summer. It contained pictures of crops at various stages, methods used, successes and suggestions for improvement. They explained that throughout summer and into fall, crops were harvested and used by elementary school students participating in the Design Center's Cooking and Nutrition Program. These youngsters made salsas, jams and jellies, and other food products which, along with fresh vegetables, were sold at farmer's markets, the Living Green Expo, Garden Resource Fair and State Fair Eco Experience. Thousands of people therefore enjoyed the efforts of these youngsters.

The Garden Corps Program employs 24 young persons each summer to plant and maintain its seven gardens. Additionally, 100 young people in kindergarten through high school engage in hands-on gardening and maintenance experiences through the Design Center's Youth Enterprise in Food and Ecology project. The efforts of these youngsters have served to beautify and revitalize their community.

Ellie Bruner

Note: The Community Design Center has been renamed Urban Roots.

Children's Museum Art park

The Minnesota Children's Museum, located in downtown Saint Paul, built an elaborate ArtPark on its rooftop in 2003 with the aim of "merging nature and art". The Saint Paul Garden Club awarded $2,000 toward the project, with club member Joan Duddingston sponsoring the museum's request.

The park operates from Memorial Day into fall. It provides a gazebo, a pond and stream for creative play with water, a dry and wet sand bed, and opportunities to experiment with wind and to grow plants.

Surrounded by the downtown skyline, visitors engage in various projects that expose them to green concepts through creative means. The juxtaposition between urban and natural landscapes produces a truly unique atmosphere in which both children and adults can interact with nature and art.

Located in Saint Paul since 1995, the children's museum first opened in downtown Minneapolis in 1981. As attendance grew, it moved to Bandana Square in Saint Paul four years later and to downtown Saint Paul in 1995.

Angel Crandall

Gillette Children's Hospital

The Gillette State Hospital for Crippled Children was built in Saint Paul's Phalen Park in 1911. One could speculate that the grounds needed renewal 51 years later, when, in 1962, the Saint Paul Garden Club donated "a substantial sum of money" to help beautify the landscape of the hospital playground.

Funds were used to purchase shrubs and trees, including three kinds of dogwood, Russian olive, golden elder, ginkgo, mountain ash, weeping willow, Norway pine, spruce and many others. The donation also funded plants for an on-site arboretum. Garden club members helped label each of the specimens to educate the youngsters about Minnesota plant life.

The hospital, renamed Gillette Children's Hospital, moved to its current location adjoining Regions Hospital near the State Capitol grounds in 1977. In 1987, the garden club again supported the hospital, donating $600 for planters. The gift was received through the Gillette Children's Hospital Foundation.

Pam Nuffort

A Profile

Charlotte Drake, Lover of Horticulture

Charlotte Drake joined the Saint Paul Garden Club in 1980 shortly
after moving from the East Coast back home to Minnesota, where she'd
grown up on Manitou Island in White Bear Lake. A widow with three
children, she married insurance executive Carl B. Drake, Jr., himself a
widower and the father of four, whom she described as "my handsome
prince on a white horse."

Charlotte wasted no time cultivating friendships within the club
and sharing her expertise on everything from vegetable gardening
to floral design. Developing members' appreciation for edible plants
was a high priority for Charlotte. "When we had flower shows in the fall, we always had vegetables,"
Ingrid Conant remembered. "Charlotte and Betty Tiffany were the ones with the beans, cucumbers and
tomatoes." To commemorate that aspect of her work with our club, members established the Charlotte
Drake Award. It's given to a flower show entry in the Horticulture Division that "uses fruits and/or
vegetables with exceptional visual appeal, reflecting the enthusiasm, joy and sense of fun of growing
one's produce."

Best in Show Winner

Charlotte won the Best in Show Horticulture Award in five consecutive club flower shows between
1992 and 2000. She also entered other Garden Club of America (GCA) shows. Ingrid remembered
working on an entry with Charlotte and Priscilla Brewster for the "Art en Fleurs" flower show in
Milwaukee in 2001. "We had a wooden box 3-by-3 feet, and we made a mini-maze. Charlotte made
detailed drawings of what to do. It was fun working on something like that with her because I learned so
much. And, we won!"

Faye Duvall recalled that Charlotte was among only a few participants in a workshop demonstration

Photo: Charlotte Drake (Mrs. Carl B., Jr.)

on fern propagation to actually succeed in growing her own fern from a spore. She gardened under lights in her basement in winter, where she also figured out how to grow vegetables hydroponically. She often brought baskets of her homegrown veggies to meetings, handing them out to members; one time she prepared a salad and served it at lunch. In October she brought mini pumpkins to share.

During her 25 years with the club Charlotte seldom let one go by without serving in some key position. She was president from 1996 to 1998. She was also active in the GCA at the national and zone levels, serving on the Horticulture Committee and as a horticulture judge.

Founders Fund Grant Writer

"There wasn't a thing she didn't know," said Ingrid, "nor was there a thing she couldn't do." Charlotte wrote the proposal for a GCA Founders Fund grant for restoration of the Gibbs Farm sod house. Ingrid also remembered that Charlotte's check was always the first to arrive for the club's annual Tea Dance.

Despite failing health Charlotte worked diligently to tie up every loose end in the last year of her life, even as she was losing her battle against ALS. She was determined, for example, to make her immense collection of gardening tools and other paraphernalia available for a garden club garage sale, with proceeds going to fund club flower shows. "Ellen Fridinger and I went to clean out her house of all the garden stuff," said Ingrid. "Both our cars were filled to the brim – the front seat, everything."

To honor her contribution to horticulture and to Saint Paul, the garden club established the Charlotte Hannaford Drake Scholarship at the University of Minnesota, which generously matched a $25,000 gift from SPGC members, GCA members and Charlotte's friends and family. The scholarship is awarded to a U of M student studying urban horticulture and garden design. Since 2007, $2,500 has been awarded annually.

Ingrid, who chaired the scholarship initiative, explained the honor this way: "It was because she was dynamite. In a very quiet way she got things done."

Bonnie Blodgett

41

Photo: John and Colles Larkin's historic garden in Dellwood features rare trees and colorful perennials.

Encourage the Best in Design, Creation and Development of Public and Private Gardens

Rice Park
Heart of the City

Beautifying historic Rice Park is the Saint Paul Garden Club's signature project. In 1927, the year the club was founded, the 32 members chose this park in the heart of downtown Saint Paul for their first civic project, and it remains the focus of our club's beautification efforts today.

This "old world" park is the heart of the city. Business men and women enjoy lunch on benches encircling the fountain plaza, or grab a hotdog from the stand next to the statue of F. Scott Fitzgerald. Mothers with kids in tow check the Peanuts sculptures. Out-of-town guests admire the magnificent architecture of buildings surrounding the park.

Bridal parties pose for pictures in front of flower-bedecked planters and hanging baskets. In the evening, people rush from nearby restaurants across the tree-lit park to plays and concerts. And, in winter, families

enjoy the adjacent ice-skating rink and marvel at the Winter Carnival ice sculptures.

The park is named for an early Minnesota senator, Henry M. Rice, who donated the land in Saint Paul's downtown district for a public park in 1849 – just one year after this region became the Minnesota Territory. By 1921, three of the city's most significant buildings bordered Rice Park: the Romanesque Revival Federal Courts building, now Landmark Center (1902); the Italian Renaissance Revival Saint Paul Hotel (1910); and the Renaissance Revival Public Library (1917) with the adjoining James J. Hill Reference Library (1921). The Ordway Center for the Performing Arts completed the square in 1985.

Photo: Saint Paul's first public park, Rice Park, in the 1920s

Yet, when the garden club got involved in 1927, the park suffered from neglect and bootleggers were living in the Saint Paul Hotel across the street.

"Imagine 32 club members armed with spades and 1,700 tulip bulbs descending on Rice Park in the fall of 1927…." wrote Jean Haut. "Perhaps they chose the tulip because it is the world's most easily recognized and most popular of all garden flowers….We wonder if they dug all of the holes themselves and what stylish outfits they would have been wearing."

Getting the tulip bulbs to rebloom was a problem. "After one season the tulips withered away and, when the next spring came, they were forgotten," according to a 1960s article by Geraldine Thompson (Mrs. Horace). The club didn't give up, however. In 1932, 1935 and 1938, members bought as many as 1,000 tulip bulbs for the park. Still, Rice Park declined, according to Geraldine:

"… for many years it was a badly kept city square through which hundreds of people passed every day on their way to the public library, the auditorium, the post office, etc." By the 1950s the park was so rundown city leaders proposed making it into a parking lot.

Fortunately, the city charter said it can never be used for anything other than a city square.

It appears the garden club's efforts to improve the park were sporadic until the early 1990s. Every few decades, club members noted

Downtown was looking shabby and launched another effort to beautify the area. In 1950, members planted 1,000 tulips at the entrance to the library. In 1956, we planted petunias downtown, which led some people to declare (unofficially) the petunia as the city's flower.

Rice Park Transformed

Between 1963 and 1968, the club allocated $200 a year "to restore and maintain Rice Park." We supported activities of the Women's Institute of Saint Paul, which in 1965 spearheaded a major renovation of the park. The institute donated the park's dramatic centerpiece, a fountain with the Alonzo Hauser bronze sculpture "The Source," which is set within a circular plaza.

Garden club member Agnes Ridder, wife of Saint Paul Dispatch-Pioneer Press publisher B.H. Ridder, Sr., was the institute's executive director. "She has traveled extensively

Photo: Bonnie Hollibush and Joan Duddingston helped plant the new south garden in 2010.

45

and came to envy the city squares and small parks she had seen in Europe," Geraldine Thompson wrote. "She determined to organize something similar in Saint Paul's Rice Park. Our club was a large contributor to her project...."

The garden club has gardened continuously in Rice Park since 1993, spending more than $37,000 on improvements. During Priscilla Brewster's 1992-95 stint as chair of the Rice Park Committee, the club added several gardens. Sally Ross, a garden designer, designed the improvements and led plantings by club members. Sally Ross credits Sally Kling for calling upon the Saint Paul Parks and Recreation Department to discuss a possible plan for Rice Park in 1992. The two Sallys had discussed how "forlorn and shabby" the city looked and the need to make improvements. Sally Ross, together with Patti Bratnober (Saunders), Mary Ann Hill and Catherine Nicholson, assessed the park's needs and Sally reported

at the club's 1992 Annual Meeting. Sally Ross's design created a sweeping hosta garden bisected by an existing water fountain, at the northern, Fifth Street, end of the park. The bed was edged with Taunton Japanese yews and White Lights azaleas.

Hosta Garden Emerges

Work began in spring 1993. "We just plain dug in and worked as hard as can be for two days," Sally recalled. "I remember being so tired; but there was such a satisfaction in the accomplishment. Diane Emerson was a great help; she was so knowledgeable. Patti Bratnober (Saunders), Lucy Dunning and other members helped plant. We bought a lot of the big-leaf, rather standard hostas, and Diane dug lovely hostas from her garden so we could have some beautiful specimens."

The following year the club created a small garden at the south end of the park behind an existing cement apron and two benches. The garden featured a Red Splendor crabapple tree, Japanese yews and White

Lights azaleas. Later, the club began planting four large (and ugly) cement planters on the plaza. In 2001, city parks provided replacements – eight attractive glazed terra cotta planters.

Every spring since then, club members have designed and planted the containers with colorful flowers and foliage. Betsy Kelly and Sally Brown purchased eight metal topiary forms to add height to the containers in 2005. Every fall, members decorate the containers with evergreen and

Photo: Containers of colorful flowers planted by our garden club ring the Rice Park fountain plaza, backed by the Saint Paul Hotel.

birch boughs, red-twigged dogwood and such. We also maintain the gardens from spring into fall.

Coordinating these volunteer efforts since 1992 has been a string of energetic Rice Park Committee chairs: Priscilla Brewster, Joan Duddingston, Roddie Turner, Sally Brown, Betsy Kelly, Marge Hols, Lucy Gehan and, currently, Becky Diekmann, Karen Neset and Shari Wilsey.

Joan Duddingston reported that in 1996 club members planted the peace garden, a small semi-circular plot with a multi-lingual incised pole, across from the Ordway Center. In 2011, Shari Wilsey and her committee planted this garden with Stella Supreme daylilies, purple fountain grass and flowering annuals.

Betsy Kelly and Sally Brown reported that our club joined the Rice Park Association in 1998-99 "to strengthen our ties with the park." The association, made up of businesses and institutions located on or near the park, helps pay for hanging baskets on decorative lampposts in the park and around Downtown.

In a major park renovation in 2001, steps on the fountain plaza were removed to make the area handicapped accessible. "We received seven flats of plants from Minnesota Green, but could not plant until

August," Sally Brown noted. "Once the renovations are completed, we will hold our September club meeting in the park…."

By 2009, the 15-year-old south garden needed renovation. The board allocated $10,000 to supplement a long-held $5,000 grant for Rice Park beautification from a former club member, Eunice Butler (Mrs. Francis D.). Joan Duddingston pledged the remaining $1,618 needed. City landscape architect Ellen Stewart and Marge Hols designed the new garden with help from an ad hoc committee including Sally Brown, Ellie Bruner, Joan Duddingston, Lucy Gehan and Sally Ross.

The new garden, sheltered by our Red Splendor crab, defines the south end of the park. It features a semi-circular walk with benches bordering a 40-foot garden. In 2010, Bluhm Brothers Landscaping installed the walk and garden bed. About 20 garden club volunteers, led by Marge Hols, braved two chilly, rainy mid-September mornings to plant the garden with small arborvitae, perennials and spring bulbs. A bronze plaque provided by the garden club and set into the walk reads: " 'And then my heart with pleasure fills, and dances with the daffodils.' –William Wordsworth. This

Photo: The peace garden got a redo in 2011 by Bonnie Hollibush, Ellie Bruner and Becky Diekmann.

garden is a gift from the Saint Paul Garden Club, 2010."

Each June since 2000, Rice Park has come alive with 50,000 school children and families gathering for the Flint Hills International Children's Festival. Our garden club has granted $3,000 to the sponsoring organization, the Ordway Center for the Performing Arts. Funds were used to buy plants for a Storytime Garden installation in the adjacent Hamm Plaza.

In 2013, our Rice Park co-chairs are busy making plans to renovate the hosta garden, using a $4,558 allocation from the club. New Tina crabapple trees and hostas and automatic irrigation are in our near future.

Rice Park was named "one of 10 Great Public Spaces for 2011" by the American Planning Association. "Rice Park's splendor stems from its simplicity and permanence," the association stated. "It provides a visual and physical respite from the impressive collection of buildings and busy street life that surround it." The association credited "the support of dedicated citizens" as well as creative city planning for "ensuring the longevity and vitality of a community treasure."

"The support of dedicated citizens": that's all of us in the Saint Paul Garden Club.

Marge Hols

Ash Trees at the Ordway
Through contributions of the Saint Paul Garden Club, 17 magnificent ash trees were planted on Fifth and Washington Streets in Saint Paul in front of the Ordway Center for the Performing Arts after the theater opened in 1985. This effort has enriched the urban environment for generations of Ordway patrons and visitors to the area. Garden club members pictured are Tottie Lilly and Clover Earl with Carl Drake, Jr. (husband of Charlotte Drake), who celebrated the event with a groundbreaking ceremony.

Tracy Stutz

A Profile

Daisy Thomson Abbott, 1930s Garden Columnist

"Brightening the home surroundings" during the 1930s Depression is what English-born horticulturalist Daisy Thomson Abbott set out to do with her Sunday *Pioneer Press* column "Our Minnesota Garden," her two books, magazine articles and her lectures – and that is what she did.

Daisy married Minnesotan Dr. John Steele Abbott while he was serving with the British forces in World War I, and returned with him to Saint Paul in 1919. The family lived at 19 Crocus Place, where Daisy planted a sunny garden in front and a steep hillside garden in the back.

Daisy joined the Saint Paul Garden Club in 1934 and was an active member until 1943. She was also a member of the Minnesota Garden Flower Society and Garden Club of Ramsey County, and chaired the Women's Institute of Saint Paul.

Northern Gardening

How did an English gardener become an American garden writer? "When I came to this country from England," she explained, "I found that I could not grow plants as I had done at home, conditions were so different." She took horticulture classes at the University of Minnesota to learn more about gardening in a climate with freezing winters and "dry" (to an Englishwoman) summers.

Then, in 1931, after phone calls from her club members summoned her in repeatedly from the garden, Daisy "in a bad temper" wrote out some answers to their questions and sent them to the *Pioneer Press*. She was promptly offered a job. Daisy began to write "especially for the housewife who does her own gardening in odd moments and likes to do it with a minimum of expense and back-breaking." Defending her adopted country from a Dutch critic who "thinks the people of America are only interested in 'going places', and that they should grow more gardens as an interest to keep them away from crime," Daisy exclaimed, "I wish he could see my weekly mail on the subject of growing gardens.

Photo: Daisy Thomson Abbott (Mrs. John S.)

I feel sure that he would realize that in Saint Paul, at any rate, everyone hurries home to dig, and that our surroundings are growing more beautiful every year. Why there is hardly a home, however small, which has not some kinds of blossoms around it...."

Daisy's sense of humor and vigorous writing style show especially well in her many charming lead sentences: "Why not water the garden rather than the sidewalk?" "Such lovely weather. Let us get out and kill something, as the Englishman says! A bug hunt...." "A dog in your garden! And why not?"

'Answer to Bleeding Heart'

In her popular columns, Daisy also solved her readers' particular gardening problems. She often gave each correspondent an identifying nickname, such as "Answer to Old Girl," "Answer to Muddled," "Answer to Dripping Roof " and "Answer to Bleeding Heart." Still "besieged" with "oft-repeated" questions, Daisy begged, "Oh! Neighbors, have a heart! How can anyone work on gardens and answer the telephone all the time? Why not read the little book; most of the answers to your ever-recurring problems will be found in it."

The "little book" was Daisy's gardening guide for Minnesota gardeners, first written as a 50-cent pamphlet and then published by the University of Minnesota Press in 1938 as *The Northern Garden Week by Week*. It gave "particular attention to those plants which will grow in the northern climate without too much care" and was the "first garden book to be written especially for the Northern states." Some of her advice is alarmingly dated, such as "... get a can of arsenate of lead mixed with tobacco...." or "The mosquitos [sic] have arrived: Do you know that they hate kerosene? Smear some on your arms...." But it is always amusing, for instance when she advised killing mealy bugs by painting each one with half water and half alcohol: "He doesn't like it at all, is probably a prohibitionist!" Her 1939 book, *The Indoor Gardener,* is packed with confidence-building, and still useful, advice about how to grow houseplants.

"It is most interesting," replied Daisy to a reader who thanked her for sharing her gardening wisdom, "to write of what we love."

Nancy Scherer

Photo, from left: Daisy Abbott with Margaret Wright (Mrs. Cushing F.) and Kathleen Gates (Mrs. Stanley) in 1935.

Minnesota Landscape Arboretum
An Inspiration for All

Established in 1958 in Chanhassen, the Minnesota Landscape Arboretum is a magnificent tract of land encompassing marshland, rolling hills and ravines as well as the remnants of an oak-maple-basswood forest. This acreage, now including a planted prairie, a wetland restoration called the spring peeper meadow and an oak savannah, is an accumulation of properties acquired over time according to need and availability. Although administered separately, the arboretum is part of the University of Minnesota's Department of Horticultural Science.

The Men's Garden Club of Minneapolis initiated a drive to create the arboretum in 1955 and enlisted the help of the Minnesota State Horticultural Society to raise funds. But it was the ladies of the Lake Minnetonka Garden Club who actually raised most of the initial money to purchase land. Lake Minnetonka provided funds for the original land acquisition in 1958 and our Saint Paul club members subsequently pledged funds for an early addition of land. Both clubs are members of the Garden Club of America, which was among the first to recognize the arboretum's potential. In May 1959, the GCA presented its prestigious Founders Fund Award to the Lake Minnetonka club for the arboretum, a $2,500 stipend for a landscape study and plan.

Our club got involved once it was evident more land than the original parcel of 160 acres was required for the arboretum's expanding collections. In 1963, Charlotte Ordway (Mrs. John G., Sr.) led club members to commit

Photo: The Saint Paul Garden Club sponsored the Woodland Azalea Garden in 1984.

to the purchase of the 97-acre farm of Ray and Caroline Williams, thereby doubling the arable acreage of the arboretum.

The arboretum's stated mission is three-pronged: "…to provide a community and a national resource for horticultural and environmental information, research and public education; to develop and evaluate plants and horticultural practices for cold climates; and to inspire and delight all visitors with quality plants in well-designed and maintained displays, collections, model landscapes and conservation areas."

Now encompassing 1,137 acres, the arboretum boasts control over its watershed and offers a display of over 5,000 plant species and varieties suitable to a northern climate. Because the coldest temperatures in the country normally occur in the Upper Midwest, this location offers unparalleled opportunity for horticultural research in the creation and development of cold-hardy varieties. This research was begun by the university in the late 19th century and carried forward at its Fruit

Breeding Farm and, subsequently, the Horticultural Research Center, which merged with the arboretum in 1985. It has produced many significant introductions.

Focus on Developing Cold-Hardy Plants

The initial research focus was on winter-hardy fruits. Apple varieties remain the most generally recognized, although plums, blueberries, strawberries and other fruits were introduced. The Haralson apple, introduced in 1922, is currently responsible for 50 percent of Minnesota's annual production and the Honeycrisp™ apple, introduced in 1991, is widely grown around the world.

One success story in breeding winter-hardy ornamentals is the Northern Lights series of azaleas, with its dependable flower-bud hardiness, floral abundance, fragrance and cultivars of many colors. Pink Northern Lights, the first of 13 hybrids, was introduced in 1978. Other shrub and tree introductions have become mainstays in our northern gardens, including Cardinal and Isanti dogwood and Northwood maple.

The arboretum provided space for living collections and display gardens where developing winter-hardy and disease-resistant varieties

Photo, from left: Plant Breeder Harold Pellett, former Arboretum Director Leon Snyder and Mrs. Vera Snyder, and garden club members Alice Harrison, Julie Titcomb and Tottie Lilly toured the Arboretum in 1987.

could be observed as well as tested for invasiveness. The panoply of display gardens offers a wide range of plants to the home gardener, including annuals, dwarf conifers, herbs, hostas, native plants, perennials, roses, shade trees and shrubs.

The non-circulating Andersen Horticultural Library is a resource for the ardent student/professor and gardener/nurseryman, specializing in horticulture, plant sciences, landscape design and natural history. It preserves almost 20,000 volumes that include rare botanicals as well as nearly 60,000 seed and nursery catalogues dating from 1828.

Steadfast Support from Our Club

The Saint Paul Garden Club and its members, despite being located "on the other side of the world" from Chanhassen, have been steadfast supporters of the arboretum. Since its early years, we have contributed substantially to its emergence as a significant repository of living collections at this northern latitude. On February 6, 1958, the deed for the original tract of land was presented to President Morrill and the University's Board of Regents simultaneously with a $25,000 check for the initial development of the arboretum. Records vary, but it seems the donors included private individuals and garden clubs throughout the state affiliated with the Minnesota State Horticultural Society, including our garden club. In 1961 our club was awarded a Bronze Medal by the horticultural society for promotion and support of the arboretum.

Since 1960 donations from our club have amounted to more than $50,000. These monies, when directed, have gone to display gardens, horticultural research and education. In addition, club members raised $45,000 to purchase the 97-acre addition and a $1,000 campaign overrun that was assigned to the azalea breeding project.

Our club's love affair with azaleas at the arboretum began in 1959 and '60 when the club first sponsored the azalea and rhododendron collection. More than 1,000 plants representing 70 species, varieties and hybrid seedlings were planted – the most extensive collection in the North Central Region. Over the next decade our club contributed $10,000 to maintaining the collection. In 1984 the club sponsored the Woodland Azalea Garden.

In the early 1990s, our club provided funds for an educational outreach program that focused on elementary school children in the inner city and metropolitan area. The program provided plant science lessons with professional instruction in a novel way: a customized van dubbed "The Plantmobile." The club supported the arboretum's horticulture therapy program and sensory garden, providing substantial gifts for purchasing tools, equipment and supplies. We also gave several grants to the arboretum's Center for the Development of Hardy

Plants. At the millennium, the club supported an heirloom gardens project and donated funds for a new visitor center.

Display Gardens and a Special Archive

Several of our members and/or their families have either made outright gifts or donated the major

portion of funds for display gardens. These are: the Hella and Bill Hueg Lilac Collection, the Clotilde Irvine Sensory Garden, the Elizabeth Carr Slade Perennial Garden and the Japanese Garden: "Seisui-Tei, The Garden of Pure Water," donated by

John and Marge Ordway.

Four members of our club, Priscilla Brewster, Charlotte Drake, Catherine Nicholson and Mary Stanley, served three three-year appointments on the arboretum Board of Trustees. Although they served as individuals, they kept the club engaged in arboretum projects.

Our garden club has a special link to the arboretum's Andersen library through another former member, Frannie Williams. Frannie was an avid horticulturalist. She grew and bred hostas for over 40 years, taking copious notes and corresponding worldwide. The popular hybridized Frances

Williams Hosta is her creation and was registered and introduced in 1986.

Our Minnesota Landscape Arboretum is a well-loved "Northern Treasure," and our garden club is proud to have made meaningful contributions to such an amazing place.

Colles Larkin

Note: This information is drawn largely from the archives of the Saint Paul Garden Club, Minnesota State Horticultural Society and the Minnesota Landscape Arboretum's Andersen Horticultural Library, as well as Susan Davis Price's book, *Northern Treasure, The Minnesota Landscape Arboretum and Horticultural Research Center*, Afton Historical Society Press, 2008.

Photos, from left: Clotilde Irvine Sensory Garden; and Frannie Williams and Hella Hueg: "We didn't plan to wear the same dress!"

Marion Fry, Making Music in our Landscapes

Marion Fry (Mrs. Robert), a landscape designer, was transplanted from San Francisco to Saint Paul in 1954. She joined the Saint Paul Garden Club in 1960 and jumped right into the activities, co-chairing a club flower show in 1961. She received the Garden Club of America Zone XI Horticulture Award in 1993. She continued her membership for more than 40 years until 2002.

Growing up on an orange ranch in Fullerton, California, Marion was exposed at an early age to gardening and flower arranging. Her father loved genetics and experimented with cross-breeding plants. Her mother taught Japanese flower arrangement. Marion studied art, ceramics and metal work in junior college, and then transferred to the University of California at Berkeley to study art and architecture. "Then, because a 'lady' architect's chances of employment seemed slim in 1929-1933, I switched to occupational therapy," she wrote.

Marion later returned to landscaping. In the Twin Cities, she began designing residential landscapes in 1959. "I place emphasis upon uses of the space, indoor-outdoor access, architectural elements of the garden and plant material," she wrote. "I especially design decks, fences, terraces, etc. – structural elements of the garden."

"Twin Cities homeowners came to admire Marion's ability to create harmony between a house and its terrain," according to a 1994 article in *Midwest Home and Design*. "I think about how clients live on and in their property. My specialty is looking at the whole package. I try to design what they really want, even if they don't know what that is," she said.

One of Marion's clients was Sally Ross, who engaged Marion for design work in her yard in 1963. The two became friends, and Sally says it was Marion who inspired her to study landscape design at the University of Minnesota and launch her own career as a garden designer.

Photo: Marion Fry (Mrs. Robert)

As a further help to homeowners, Marion wrote a book, *A Space of One's Own: The Lively Process of Personal Landscape Design*, which was published in 1992 by the Andersen Horticultural Library at the Minnesota Landscape Arboretum. The book describes fundamentals of landscape design and Marion's ideas, and gives examples of landscape projects.

After Marion and Robert "built two houses on very steep hills in California," they chose steep lots here in Saint Paul, too. Marion designed "a meadow on a hill" behind the Fry's home, planting wildflowers and native grasses. She garnished the front of her home with window boxes and pots of flowers. As she told a *Midwest Home* writer, "A home should be a haven and a garden should make music."

Deni Svendsen

56

Blooming Saint Paul
Beautifying Our Community

Inspired by the Grow Chicago program and transformation of Chicago's Miracle Mile into a spectacular linear garden, members of the Saint Paul Garden Club initiated a multi-year effort in 2000 to beautify downtown Saint Paul. Their advocacy and leadership helped spawn the cooperative Blooming Saint Paul program, which has transformed not only Downtown, but streets, parks and neighborhoods throughout the city. Today, nearly 500 hanging baskets, dozens of planters and an array of public and private gardens at 120 sites decorate the city. More than 400 people volunteer in the city's parks.

The garden club continues to co-sponsor the program, providing volunteer help from members and funds to purchase plants for seasonal displays in large urns on the Kellogg Boulevard medians downtown. Impact of the displays goes beyond

beautification, according to Mark Granlund, who coordinates Blooming Saint Paul. "It's been educational, too," he said. "Downtown businesses have asked what is planted in the urns so they could repeat the look in their own plazas. The plant palette for downtown has become much more varied and sophisticated."

What follows is the story of

the garden club's leadership and participation in Blooming Saint Paul. In June 1999, garden club members Betsy Kelly and Paula Soholt traveled to Chicago for a gardening conference and were inspired by the gardening and beautification happening under Mayor Richard Daley's leadership. Betsy approached the city of Saint Paul about transforming downtown

Photo: Displays of colorful flowers and ornamental grasses decorate Kellogg Boulevard in downtown Saint Paul.

with plantings, baskets and urns.

To build excitement and gain support for beautifying Saint Paul, the garden club organized a meeting in April 2000 at Landmark Center with the support of Mayor Norman Coleman. The guest speakers were key people in the development of the Grow Chicago program, landscape architect Douglas Hoerr and Chicago Park District Chief of Staff Drew Becher.

Green Spaces Foster Community

Club members worked hard to promote the project, but plans didn't advance much until 2002, after the election of Mayor Randy Kelly and subsequent appointment of Bob Bierscheid as Director of Parks and Recreation. Both men were aware of the Chicago program and saw the benefits of beautifying downtown Saint Paul. They were inspired by University of Illinois research showing that "Green spaces contribute to a healthier environment and foster

a sense of community," which, in turn, "leads residents to feel safer and behave more civilly towards one another."

The city decided to plant the medians along three blocks of Kellogg Boulevard on the Mississippi River bluff between the Robert Street

and Wabasha Street bridges. Plans included in-ground beds, 11 urns and irrigation throughout. Mark Madsen of Bachman's created the design in partnership with Tim Agness and Jody Martinez of the city's Parks and Recreation Design Section.

To help pay for the project,

the garden club, led by Betsy Kelly, prepared an application for a STAR (State Tax Revitalization) grant from the city, assisted by Paula Soholt, Joan Duddingston and Deni Svendsen. The garden club pledged $10,000 in matching funds and volunteer labor of $5,000. Thanks to support from Mayor Kelly and the city council, a three-year grant totaling $205,000 was awarded to our garden club as funding partner. The years of 2003-04 saw many advances in city beautification. The medians along Kellogg Boulevard were planted and plantings at City Hall were improved and expanded. Mark Granlund was promoted to Arts and Gardens Coordinator for Parks and Recreation to oversee maintenance and development of gardening activities. Garden club members met frequently with Mark to develop the Blooming Saint Paul program, which began officially in 2003.

There was a groundswell of

Photo, from left: Paula Soholt, Mayor Chris Coleman and Betsy Kelly

58

interest in beautifying Downtown through attractive plantings. At the mayor's request, a contingent from the city attended a Greening Conference in Chicago. Representing our garden club were Paula Soholt and Deni Svendsen.

Once home, the group developed plans for planting a core downtown area by the city parks design section. A horticulture staff structure and budget to handle current and future workloads was devised. The Youth Job Corps program was tapped to provide three gardening crews. Around City Hall, 27 window-box planters and four large urns were added. Work also was done to develop partnerships and opportunities.

Baskets Decorate Streets

In 2005, a Golden Bloom Awards program was initiated by the city with our garden club as a co-sponsor (see Blooming Saint Paul Awards). Also, two programs providing hanging baskets on streetlight poles in downtown Saint Paul, begun in

1998 by Capital City Partnership and the Rice Park Association, were incorporated into Blooming Saint Paul. The program has since doubled to nearly 500 hanging baskets and is still funded mainly by community organizations.

By 2007, Blooming Saint Paul had gained notice. The program and its staff received awards and recognition from the Minnesota Recreation and Parks Association, Saint Paul City Council, Minnesota State Horticultural Society and the Garden Club of America.

Once the STAR grant ended, the garden club in 2007 began granting funds annually to the city Parks and Recreation Department to purchase plants for the program. Grants have totaled $22,225.

A 17-member Blooming Saint Paul Advisory Panel was created in 2008 at the recommendation of garden club members. Roddie Turner represents the garden club on the advisory panel, which helps guide

program activities.

Funding was a major challenge in 2009 as the city struggled to manage with reduced state financial support. Maureen Adelman, Marge Hols, Ellie Bruner and Lucy Gehan wrote letters to Mayor Chris Coleman, Parks and Recreation Department Director Mike Hahm and city council members encouraging them to continue funding for Blooming Saint Paul. Maureen met personally with Mayor Coleman. The program survived and Mark Granlund and his team are still doing annual plantings.

Today, Blooming Saint Paul is an interdepartmental city program that partners with more than 20 businesses and community groups for city beautification. Our garden club supports spin-off projects operated by some of these groups. For example, since 2006, we've granted $11,060 to the Dayton's Bluff Community Council for its Blooming Business Streets Project.

Betsy Kelly and Maureen Adelman

Blooming Saint Paul Awards
Kudos for City Gardeners

The first Golden Bloom Awards ceremony, to present the 2005 awards for outstanding public and private gardens in Saint Paul, was held in January 2006 at the Como Park conservatory. City gardeners gathered to receive and applaud winners for best residential, business/institutional, environmental and vegetable gardens. There were also awards for best garden maintained by volunteers on city property, art in the garden and outstanding gardening advocate.

The event was hosted by Bob Bierscheid, director of Saint Paul Parks and Recreation, new Mayor Chris Coleman and the Saint Paul Garden Club, with President Ingrid Conant presiding. Betsy Kelly, the garden club's "founding mother" of Blooming Saint Paul, organized the event.

Maureen Adelman, who joined the garden club later that year, won the first place Golden Bloom Award

for Art in the Garden. She said she loved the event at Como. The appetizers were cut out in the shape of flowers and two very beautiful floral arrangements made everyone in attendance realize that the talented women of the garden club hosted the event. Many of our members wore beautiful Garden Club of America scarves. Maureen wore a flowered

turban to cover her head due to chemotherapy. She and her husband Ira were surprised and excited to receive the award.

The program, renamed Blooming Saint Paul Awards, is an initiative of the Saint Paul Department of Parks and Recreation, our garden club, Ramsey County Master Gardeners, who serve as judges, and Public Art

Photo: The 2009 Residential Bronze Bloom award was won by Nancy Scherer.

Saint Paul. It is sponsored by the Saint Paul Pioneer Press. Any garden located within Saint Paul city limits can be nominated for an award in one of seven categories. Golden Bloom, Silver Bloom, Bronze Bloom awards are given for each category.

As attendance at the awards grew, the event moved to the Wellstone Center for three years and, in 2012, to Saint Thomas University. As Blooming Saint Paul chairwoman, Maureen Adelman planned the events with assistance from Lucy Gehan. Each year, about 15 members of the garden club volunteered to hostess and help serve refreshments.

Besides Maureen, four other garden club members have won awards: 2006 award, Golden Bloom for City Property, Summit Monument Garden, Marge Hols (with Jeanne Weigum). 2006 award, Gardening Advocate, Marge Hols. 2007 award, Golden Bloom for Residential Garden, Joan Duddingston. 2009 award, Bronze Bloom for Residential Garden, Nancy

Scherer. 2010 award, Gardening Advocate, Bonnie Blodgett. 2011 award, Bronze Bloom for Residential Garden, Bonnie Blodgett.

Guest speakers at the awards have included two garden club members. Marge Hols, a former *Saint Paul Pioneer Press* garden columnist, spoke in 2010, and Bonnie Blodgett, the newspaper's current garden columnist, addressed the gathering in 2011.

In 2010, Public Art Saint Paul joined the awards program, providing awards to people who are volunteer stewards for sculptures in their neighborhoods. The city's Landmark Trees Program also participates, recognizing people who nominate significant trees –"those that stand out from all the rest"– on private or public property in the city.

Maureen Adelman

Photo: A massive stone lion brings whimsy to Maureen Adelman's garden.

Como Park
Japanese Garden and Conservatory

The Saint Paul Garden Club has enjoyed an informal partnership with Como Park in Saint Paul ever since the early 1930s, when long-time park advocate Charlotte Ordway, wife of 3M Company founder John G. Ordway, served as our club president.

The park was in its sixth decade then, and hurting from the Depression. During Charlotte's tenure as president (1932-34), the ladies of the garden club worked hard to ensure that the park and its conservatory, built in 1915, would survive that challenging era. They supported the conservatory's flower shows, the park's elaborate formal gardens and the recreational activities that meant so much to the citizens of Minnesota. Hard-working immigrants had always been attracted to the park and now, more than ever, they sought out its natural beauty as a kind of spiritual refuge. It had become a favorite Saint Paul leisure destination.

Japanese Garden Created

Charlotte Ordway's passion for horticulture and her love of Como Park inspired her five children to underwrite the creation of a one-acre Japanese garden on the Como grounds in her memory. The garden was designed by Matsami Matsuda, a legendary maker of gardens and heir to a long family history in horticulture.

Construction began in 1979 and the Ordway garden was a huge hit with the public. But within a few years it was clear that it needed a makeover if it were to live up to the ideal of perfection envisioned by the exacting Matsuda. After several years of study and discussion, followed by several trips to Como Park by the master himself, the Charlotte Ordway

Photo: The serene Charlotte Partridge Ordway Japanese Garden was built in 1979.

Japanese Garden was unveiled for a second time in 1992.

The garden was updated again in 2011. The most recent rejuvenation was part of a major overhaul made possible by a capital campaign in which many garden club members played key roles.

Conservatory Restored

Minnesota's extreme climate is just as hard on buildings as it is on exotic gardens. By the end of the 20th Century, the conservatory needed major help. There had been renovations before and even a new glass roof installed, but this was different. Como's magnificent conservatory was facing demolition.

The family of another past garden club president, Marjorie McNeely, stepped up. They knew how she had loved the fine old building. Who better than Marjorie to be memorialized through its restoration? She'd served as club president in 1963-65 and a few members still fondly remember their former president's passionate love of gardening. They especially recalled the flower-arranging classes she led, often using flowers picked fresh from her extensive cutting gardens.

In December 2002, the McNeely family, organized by Marjorie's husband, Donald, agreed to underwrite a $7 million project to save (read:

rebuild) the conservatory, which reopened under its new name, the Marjorie McNeely Conservatory, in 2004.

Also in 2002, garden club member Ruth Huss and her husband, John, gave the lead gift to build a state-of-the-art orchid room to house the conservatory's extensive collection of orchids.

Between 1980 and 2009, our garden club supported a number of projects at Como Park including the Japanese garden and a rooftop garden at the new visitor center. Our most recent efforts on behalf of the park, in 2010-12, were grants totaling $5,450 from our Community Fund to support the Conservation Corps Minnesota's work on the grounds. The corps offers nominal stipends to low-income teens deployed throughout the park to do everything from collecting debris to killing buckthorn. The grants enabled the corps to replace buckthorn with hundreds of native trees.

Bonnie Blodgett

Note: Bonnie Blodgett is co-author of *Jewel of Como, The Marjorie McNeely Conservatory,* Afton Historical Press, 2009.

Photo: A wing of the Marjorie McNeely Conservatory during restoration

Governor's Residence Garden
The People's House

The gardens of the Minnesota Governor's Residence at 1006 Summit Avenue were one of the Saint Paul Garden Club's hands-on projects. This was the original home of one of our club's founding members, Clotilde McCullough Irvine.

The story begins in 1908, after newlyweds Horace and Clotilde Irvine returned from an extended European holiday. They hired architect William Channing Whitney to build their first home, incorporating many of the architectural, artistic and cultural influences they experienced during their travels. In spring 1910, Mr. Whitney completed his renderings, which included a stately English Tudor Revival home of brick and stone surrounded by Victorian gardens. The home was completed in 1912. Although those original garden plans were scaled back, the gardens still featured many traditional elements

including fences, structures of wrought iron and bronze, and noteworthy and unique plantings.

The Irvines raised their four children, Olivia, Elizabeth, Clotilde and Thomas, in the home. Known for their philanthropic endeavors and commitment to the community, the Irvines instilled those same values in their children. In 1964, Olivia and

her sister, Clotilde Irvine Moles (Mrs. Edwin J., Jr.) donated their cherished family home to the State of Minnesota (see Profile on Olivia Irvine Dodge). The home was to be "the people's house" and serve as the residence of the governor and his family.

With each new gubernatorial administration, the gardens on the property underwent phases of

Photo: Governor's Residence garden in the 1980s

64

redesign, renewal and overgrowth. Often, these were a reflection of the individual tastes and preferences of the First Ladies. In 1968, First Lady Iantha P. LeVander, with the assistance of private gifts and legislative appropriations, oversaw the selection and installation of a sculpture by Minnesota Artist Paul Granlund. The sculpture, Man-Nam, honors Minnesotans who lost their lives in Viet Nam. Mrs. LeVander also envisioned and was the impetus behind large wildflower gardens on the property.

Restoring Wildflower Gardens

In an almost seamless transition, our garden club, along with many other individuals and groups in the community, picked up where the Irvine family left off with the beautiful gardens and open spaces on the property. In 1977, our members worked hard to restore and renew the wildflower gardens started by Mrs. Levander. In our club's 1978 Annual

Report, Alice Harrison described the efforts taken to prepare the soil for the myriad new plantings, with an eye toward expanding the gardens over time. The report also documented the club's agreement with First Lady Lola

Perpich to meet every two years to review the success of the gardens. This would be a long-standing relationship, as Governor Rudy Perpich went on to become the longest serving governor in Minnesota history.

In 1980, the Minnesota Legislature established the Governor's Residence Council to prepare and adopt master plans for the residence and gardens.

The aim was to ensure that a more uniform approach would be followed in the future to avoid possible undue influence of the individual preferences of governors' families.

Under the council's guidance, in 1982, during the Quie administration, the club, along with others in the community, helped install a perennial garden on the east side of the property. For the next seven years club members made the gardens their hands-on project. They prepared the soil, planted flowers and maintained beds. The club also made a sizeable financial commitment to the gardens, spending $14,376 between 1977 and 1987 for plants, shrubs, trees and supplies.

Anxiety Over Big Project

Our club archives include a design and plan to replant a perennial garden. In their 1987-1988 Governor's Residence Committee Report, Betty Tiffany and Sally Ross summarized

Photo, back row, from left: Betty Tiffany, Mimi Davidson, Julie Titcomb, Carolyn DeCoster, Susan Lueck; front row: Helen Comfort, Sally Kling, Sally Ross and Jane Marinell, the residence groundskeeper

their work, including the following poignant entries: March 17-April 16: "About 27 days of worry for Sally and me—how can we assemble the right amount of help to dig perennials, get the tilling done, divide the plants we intend to use, replant and plant new perennials, all in one day?" April 14: "A telephone call from Lowell Bursell (residence staff gardener) put us at ease. He had removed all plants, tilled and the garden is ready for planting – an unexpected, wonderful surprise!"

April 16: "The rest of the story goes quickly because of the magnificent response of garden club members. Ten members and 3 Master Gardeners from the University Extension program planted quickly and easily in the grid Lee Driscoll had laid over the perennial bed."

A year later, our club received notice that a landscaping company was being hired to do work at the residence and our volunteer services would no longer be needed. Long-time members still talk about the disappointment this decision caused. As Faye Duvall recalled, Governor Perpich was planning for his daughter's wedding and wanted to add a terrace off the back of the house. In 1990, the governor thanked members at a reception. The club received a certificate of appreciation from the State of Minnesota and governor "for the fine efforts and beautiful contributions of club volunteers at the Governor's mansion." The club moved on, and by the early 1990s had chosen Rice Park in Downtown Saint Paul as its next hands-on gardening project (see Rice Park).

In 2012, the 100th anniversary of the residence, the Governor's Residence Council asked our club to provide garden docents for six summer house and garden tours. Ellen Fridinger, who had volunteered in the gardens years before, was joined by Maureen Adelman, Susan Brust, Brenda Hoffman, Marge Hols, Carol Kolb, Catherine Nicholson and Deb Venker. Armed with lists of plants in bloom, they introduced visitors to such beauties as the yellow 'Bartzella' Itoh Hybrid peony and stars of the hosta, iris and lily collections. They guided guests through the Children's Garden, where plaques list each governor's children. More than 2,000 visitors toured the house and garden over the summer.

Ellen Maas Pratt

Note: Some information in this article was drawn from *A Garden Inspires a Community*. This report about the Governor's Residence was written by Karine Pouliquen and Lori Schindler in 2009 for a graduate school course at the University of Minnesota. The two students helped to reorganize the club archives in 2009-10.

Photo: Julie Titcomb and Lee Driscoll celebrate the new garden.

A Profile

Lee Driscoll, Sustaining a Love of Gardening

While growing up, Elizabeth (Lee) Driscoll watched her mother, Elizabeth (Betty) Slade, and her Saint Paul Garden Club friends working in Betty's Dellwood garden and saw what a good time they were having. "There were howls of laughter,' she said, "so I thought the garden club was a wonderful club to belong to. I couldn't wait until I was old enough to experience it." Betty, who served as club president in 1953-55, was still a member in 1973 when Lee Driscoll (Mrs. W. John) joined the club.

Lee embraced organic gardening before it became trendy. "That comes from growing up on a farm," she said. We had cows, horses and eggs and chickens and all of them produced organic fertilizer that we used in the gardens in different ways…. As a young homemaker and young mother, I was expecting to use organic fertilizer in my garden. The magazines we were reading then urged us not to get involved with chemicals."

Lee remembers arguing with her parents' friends from the university about organic fertilizer being best because it replenishes the soil. "We didn't really know what chemicals would do to us. The assurances that came from the university seemed to make sense…but I still couldn't use chemical fertilizers and pesticides. It means that I have never had a neat and tidy garden because there are always little holes and bumps," she said of her Sunfish Lake garden.

An accomplished flower arranger, Lee said preparing for a flower show can be nerve-wracking. "You approached entering the show with a certain trepidation," she said, "but you wanted to be a good sport – to enter and make it fun, to have lots of competition and make it be successful. Thinking up something unusual or especially colorful or experimental is fun. The nerve-wracking part is the night before: You've got the real fresh flowers and the container isn't quite right and the mechanics are rickety and won't work. You have only a few hours before you have to pack it up for the show and then get it there in one

Photo: Lee Driscoll (Mrs. W. John)

piece."

Her most memorable arrangement? "I remember the goofy ones better than the normal ones," she said, laughing. One favorite was a duck blind—a dinner for two overlooking the river. "That was being a little silly and using John's duck hunting stuff as a background," she said. "I built the rudiments of a duck blind; it was a picnic and I set the table with printed bandanas."

Support for the Minnesota Landscape Arboretum was among the garden club's most significant contributions to the region, Lee said. "Our garden club was not the most important, but it was asked early and helped with buying the land to start the arboretum. Many of our earliest members have gardens that were given at the arboretum in memory of their interest and support: The Ordway (Japanese) Garden. The azalea garden. Part of the wildflower garden. The perennial garden." Lee is referring to the Elizabeth Carr Slade Perennial Garden, which she and John gave in memory of Lee's mother in 1980 (see Minnesota Landscape Arboretum).

In 1982, Lee received the first Roberta Galloway Gardner Award from our club president. In 1994, she received the coveted GCA Medal of Merit "for your exceptional artistic and creative abilities, for your quiet inspiration, and for your encouraging leadership and guidance." The letter to GCA recommending this award said, "Lee Driscoll is a member who has contributed in every conceivable area of our club and it is difficult to imagine the club without her participation.... She has been a member of the board and held many positions over the years. She was president 1986-87, assistant treasurer 1987-88, chairman of the Governor's Residence Committee 1990-91 and, most recently, co-chairman of the annual Tea Dance. She was responsible for bylaws revision in 1991. She is a Master Gardener and her many blue ribbons are famous. Her skills are many, her enthusiasm strong and her contributions many."

Lee credits the garden club with helping sustain members' interest in gardening. "Whatever was discovered – Minnesota plants, new varieties – we'd hear about and could put in our gardens. And, we'd get a head's up on a lot of information we probably wouldn't [have had] otherwise."

For Lee, gardening is a joy even if it does require hard work. "You spend all those hours working in your own yard making it a beautiful spot in this amazing world," she said. "You take responsibility for the plants and harvest the results; and, next year, you do it better. I would hope that we'd keep doing it ourselves and spend the time enjoying it and sharing it, making it an ongoing, sustainable part of our lives."

Colleen Hooley and Marge Hols

Landscape Plant Development Center

Breeding Hardy Plants

Look closely at mid-summer gardens of long-time Saint Paul Garden Club members and you're likely to find a bush clematis with charming purple, or blue-and-white, bell-shaped flowers.

In 2002, thanks to Mary Stanley, noted University of Minnesota woody plant breeder Dr. Harold Pellett asked members of the garden club to field-test some seedlings. They were crosses of two bush clematises, *Clematis integrifolia* and *C. hexapetala*. Dr. Pellett, who was retiring from the university, had founded the Landscape Plant Development Center in Chanhassen in 1990. He was attempting to breed a bush clematis with large, up-facing blue-and-white flowers for the center to introduce to gardeners. He succeeded, and Center Star clematis is in production.

The garden club began supporting the center's breeding work with a $1,000 grant in 1995, and granted

another $22,000 between 2000 and 2011. In 2006, Dr. Pellett led our garden club on a field trip through the center's new research station in Lake Elmo, which was evaluating the cold-hardiness of new selections of shrubs.

It takes 15 to 20 years to breed, develop and send to market a new woody landscape plant. Center introductions available in garden

centers are: Cool Splash™ bush honeysuckle, Center Glow™ ninebark and Silver Ball™ ornamental pear.

In 2012, the center's board decided to disband and move its assets to the Minnesota Landscape Arboretum, which was starting a new research and plant-breeding program.

Marge Hols

Photo: Dr. Harold Pellett with Center Glow™ ninebark.

Minnesota Woman Suffrage Garden

The Minnesota Woman Suffrage Memorial Garden – the first memorial recognizing the contributions of Minnesota women on the Capitol Mall in Saint Paul – was installed in 1999. The concept of 32 beds of native plants against a steel trellis showing the leaders and timeline of the Minnesota suffrage movement was so appealing, it won a design competition. But, once the garden was planted, reality set in. The prairie garden design proved unmanageable and the garden succumbed to weeds.

After another round of fund-raising, this highly visible public garden was renovated in 2004. The new garden's 14 lengthy island beds display drifts of perennials, ornamental grasses and shrubs featuring the colors of the suffrage movement: yellow and white with touches of purple.

The 90-foot steel trellis remains. It names 25 Minnesota women who led the fight here for a woman's right

to vote over a 74-year timeline, from 1846 to 1920. Flanking the trellis are steel tablets telling the history of the movement.

The Saint Paul Garden Club supported construction of the original garden with a grant of $5,000, according to its 1996-1997 Annual Report. When the garden needed renovating, the club stepped up again,

providing grants of $5,000 in 2004 and $1,000 in 2005. "Your initial grant of $5,000 in 2004 was the turning point in our efforts to raise sufficient funds to renovate the garden," Ruby Hunt of The Ross Group wrote to the garden club.

Picnic in the Garden

When Saint Paul Garden Club members spread vintage tablecloths

Photo: Memorial garden on the State Capitol Mall celebrates a woman's right to vote.

among the flower beds at the Minnesota Woman Suffrage Garden one sunny August day in 2005, they had more in mind than a simple summer picnic. They wanted to experience first hand the garden they'd help make possible.

The group had just heard a talk, "Flowers of the Past, a History of the Minnesota Woman Suffrage Garden," by Barbara Stuhler, the prime mover behind the original project. Barbara, an historian and retired University of Minnesota administrator, wrote the book *Gentle Warriors: Clara Ueland and the Minnesota Struggle for Woman Suffrage.*

Among the picnickers were two garden club members, Sally Ross and Marge Hols, who played key roles in restoring this historically significant garden on the State Capitol Mall.

Fundraising for the renovation was spearheaded by The Ross Group, a dozen civic-minded women organized by Sally Ross in 1992 with the mission of beautifying and improving Saint Paul. In 2003, Sally and her friends raised $25,700 from individual contributors. The group also approached the garden club for a $5,000 grant.

"I thought the suffrage memorial garden was a fabulous idea and I give Barbara Stuhler credit for it," said Sally, a member of the garden club since 1983 and a garden designer. "It seems to me it's very appropriate that it is located on the State Capitol grounds where one of the stages for getting suffrage rights for women occurred in the Minnesota Legislature. It was really a wonderful idea to honor women."

Marge Hols, who joined the garden club in 2002, was recruited by Barbara Stuhler to make sure the new garden would be sustainable. "This simple request grew, as volunteer efforts often do, into a three-year project," said Marge, a garden writer and designer. "As a volunteer, I redesigned the garden in concert with Roger Grothe of Aloha Landscaping in Mendota Heights. We eliminated some garden beds to make maintenance easier, improved the soil, and selected sturdy shrubs and perennials that could survive on a windy site in full sun. We arranged the new plants in large drifts of a single variety to give the garden more visual impact."

Marge Hols

Photo: Beds of perennials complement the steel trellis, which lists suffrage leaders.

Alexander Ramsey House
A Garden Restored

Nearly 100 years after the Alexander Ramsey House was built, the Saint Paul Garden Club was asked to restore its gardens to their original Victorian appearance. In 1971, the Minnesota Historical Society said it was confident that our club would have "a grasp of the problems to be overcome in such a restoration and a sensitive feeling for what the yard area should become."

Alexander Ramsey was the first governor of the Minnesota Territory and second governor of the state. He had purchased property at 265 South Exchange Street in the Irvine Park area of Saint Paul, and, after four years of construction, moved into the home in 1872. The property also featured several outbuildings, including a carriage house and a tool shed.

Annetta Morgan (Mrs. John E. P.) chaired our club's restoration committee. Over the winter committee members did their research and, in

April, submitted their proposed plans and budget. The historical society approved the plans as "authentic for the period and style of the house." Annetta said that "planning for the project was made easier because of the fine reference material available in the archives of the society. Letters, diaries, landscaping bills and pictures provided clues as to what the yard looked like in

the late 1800s."

Mrs. Ramsey loved flowers and plants, as reflected in her many letters to her daughter. In the spring, she eagerly awaited the warm days so that she and her "plant and seed man" could make selections for her window boxes on the front porch and her garden beds. The Governor had a particular interest in trees, judging

Photo: The Alexander Ramsey House in 1972

from his diaries.

Curved Walk Recreated

In 1972, club members recreated

the original curved walk from the side porch of the house to the carriage house, edged by a flower border. They had consulted old gardening books and catalogues to select plants that were authentic to the period, of easy maintenance and hardy in Minnesota. When they could not find the exact varieties, they chose the oldest available. In addition to a large perennial bed, the club created a small rose bed planted with twelve hybrid perpetual roses and edged with white *Iberis sempervirens* (candytuft). Club records also refer to planting of peonies, pinks, geraniums and *Dictamnus* (gas plant).

Around the house, our members separated and replanted lilies of the valley and hostas. At the front door, they replaced some of the *Spiraea* x *vanhouttei* (a type of bridal-wreath spirea). To the left of the porch steps, they planted a group of *Spiraea sorbifolia* (ash leaf spirea) and, on the right, a globe arborvitae. They also planted snowberry bushes, *Taxus cuspidata* (upright Japanese yew) and five French hybrid lilacs, which were introduced in the United States toward the end of the 19th Century.

Favorite Trees Planted

Near the drawing room window went a *Prunus triloba* (flowering almond) and near the dining room window a mountain ash, one of the Governor's favorite trees. The ash was surrounded by a large bed of various native ferns, grown and donated by a club member. Although the location was not specified, the club also planted flowering crab, Japanese tree lilac, viburnum and a large arborvitae. In the fall, our members planted spring-flowering bulbs.

The club contributed to the project all of the plant material, at a cost in excess of $2,200. Moreover, with the exception of digging the beds and border and planting the larger trees and shrubs, the members did all of the work. That included planting 800 square feet of flower beds and laying 1,600 Belden bricks along the asphalt walkway and around the flower beds. The club also contributed funding for a part-time gardener to provide maintenance for the project's first year.

Restoration of the Ramsey House gardens was another example of the Saint Paul Garden Club's long-standing commitment to fostering an appreciation for gardening in the public spaces of the city.

Anne Ferrell

Photo: Garden Club members recreated the original brick walk in 1972. From left: Betty Slade, Marion Fry and Betty Biorn

YWCA Japanese Garden

Bringing Cultures Together

At one time, Saint Paul had two Japanese gardens. One was inside, the YWCA Japanese Garden at 65 Kellogg Boulevard; and one outside, the Ordway Japanese Garden at Como Park. Both gardens opened in 1972 and both were supported by the Saint Paul Garden Club.

The YWCA garden, created by volunteers, "included a waterfall and small bridge, evergreens, ground covers, birch trees, dogwood, Japanese lanterns and logs to sit on," according to an article in the *Saint Paul Pioneer Press* on June 11, 1973. The article described the dedication of the garden to Ruth Tanbara, an exceptional woman of Japanese heritage who had retired after 30 years on the YWCA staff.

Mrs. Tanbara and her husband, Earl, moved to Saint Paul in 1942 from California to find jobs and homes for Japanese Americans who

were removed from their West Coast homes during World War II. At a time of hysteria against Oriental-looking people, the Tanbaras had been given 48-hours notice by the government to leave their home—a dark period in our history. If they could show support for themselves and move inland they could bypass the relocation camps. They sold everything they had and

came to Saint Paul by train. Ruth lived a long and productive life, involved not only in the YWCA, but in many Saint Paul organizations. She died in 2008 at the age of 100, a beloved and honored woman.

In 1990 the YWCA building was sold and the Paul and Sheila Wellstone Elementary School moved into the building. The garden

Photo: YWCA Japanese Garden was dedicated to long-time staff member Ruth Tanbara in 1973.

remained for the students to enjoy Japanese culture and learn about a Japanese-American woman who contributed greatly to our community. In the summer of 2010 the Wellstone School moved to new quarters. Currently, there are no plans for the building, according to staff of the Saint Paul Public School Facilities Planning Department. The staff said they did not know if the garden still exists.

The YWCA moved to new quarters at 375 Selby Avenue in 1990. In 1993, two members of the Saint Paul Garden Club who were longtime supporters of the YWCA, Betty Tiffany and Julie Titcomb, decided to establish an indoor container garden in the atrium at the new location. The garden club gave $1,250 for plants and help with heavy lifting. Later, the atrium was used for health and fitness facilities. The container garden was given to DARTS, which provides accessible transportation and community services in Dakota County.

Carolyn DeCoster

Photo, from left: Carolyn DeCoster, Betty Tiffany and Julie Titcomb created an indoor container garden at the YWCA in 1993.

Phalen Lake Poetry Park
Growing a Magic Dragon

With a stony eye, nostrils crawling with wooly thyme and a mouth of fiery red celosia plumes, it's a face only a child or a gardener could love.

"Kids know right away it's a dragon, although often adults don't," Mem Lloyd said of the garden, which is located in Saint Paul's Phalen Lake Poetry Park.

Lloyd, an art teacher, designed the garden. She is a board member of the East Side Arts Council, which pulled together resources to build the garden and adjacent Poet's Post in 1998. The Saint Paul Garden Club supported the project with grants totaling $6,000 in 2000 and 2001.

Garden whimsy at its best, the 60-foot dragon sits on a grassy berm, its body curled into a U-shape so its tail nearly meets its head. You can walk into its belly, a pea gravel-floored "room" complete with benches shaped like open books. "It's wonderful to see

the kids come through, go from stone to stone and play on it," Lloyd said. "They come back and say, 'This is my special place.'"

Nearby, poetry is displayed on a Poet's Post. "The idea was some child could take her Grandpa to the park and say, 'I wrote this poem,'" said Kitty Anderson, a fellow arts council board member. Poems by Maria Olofsdotter

were on display when I visited the garden in 2002.

The dragon wears a creative ensemble of shrubs, perennials, annuals and ornamental grasses. Tall tufts of variegated feather reed grass project like armor along its back and creeping junipers simulate its scaly sides.

Marge Hols

Photo: Poetry Park's 60-foot floral dragon enchanted children.

Historic Larkin Garden

Documented in Archives of American Gardens

The enchanting 1920s walled garden of Colles and John Larkin in Dellwood was chosen for inclusion in the Archives of American Gardens at the Smithsonian Institution in Washington, D.C., in 2006. Colles Larkin is a long-time member of the Saint Paul Garden Club, which nominated the garden.

The archives preserve photographs and descriptions that document garden design in America. They provide scholars, researchers and others with visual documentation of cultural, historical and vernacular gardens. The Garden Club of America, which has a collection within the archives, encourages its member clubs to nominate significant gardens.

The Larkin garden, built in 1928, features a Normandy-style stone house, once a pool house, and an 85-foot swimming pool enclosed in a garden with massive limestone

and fieldstone walls. Stone stairways ascend to a woodland garden with pathways that meander around long beds of perennials. A sunken, circular gathering place is centered by an 1880s fountain. A brick-paved overlook provides a place to sit and enjoy an elevated view of the house and pool. Exotic trees, John Larkin's passion, are planted throughout the garden.

Colles favors her kitchen garden, where she's transformed "long boring rows" into a charming parterre enclosed by stone walls, the house and a fence with a gate and arbor garnished with morning glories. Herbs fill a central circular bed and dwarf Korean lilac standards anchor the four corners. Four L-shaped and four rectangular beds house a variety of fruits and

Photo: The Larkin's Normandy-style home and walled garden

vegetables including strawberries, asparagus, beets and butternut squash. Dahlias and old-fashioned hollyhocks brighten a long bed beside the house.

Our garden club also nominated The Garth at House of Hope Presbyterian Church on Saint Paul's

historic Summit Avenue for the archives. The garden, designed by Ann McMillan, was accepted in 2002.

The Garth, an inner courtyard, is "a quiet garden setting for reflection and prayer," according to the church. The Garth includes a columbarium where church members may intern cremated remains of their families.

Marge Hols

Photo, clockwise from left: Sisters-in-law Leslie Carnes (left) and Jean Rowland Engle proposed The Garth for the Smithsonian Archives; John and Colles Larkin; 1880s fountain; and stone stairway to upper Larkin garden

Saint Paul Parks Conservancy

Expanding City Parks

The Saint Paul Parks Conservancy was founded in 2008 with a mission of enhancing and expanding parks and recreational opportunities in Saint Paul.

The conservancy was organized in response to a study conducted by the City of Saint Paul to identify desirable enhancements to parks and recreational opportunities. The study resulted in hiring a consultant, funded by the McKnight Foundation in 2008 and 2009, to establish the conservancy, recruit a board of directors and define a mission. The conservancy received nonprofit status in April of 2008. While independent in its choice of projects, it embraces the city's 2008 Parks and Recreation Vision Plan. The conservancy board consists of 12 volunteer members. Two are Saint Paul Garden Club members: Priscilla Brewster, chair in 2008-12; and Marge Hols, secretary. A third club member,

Ingrid Conant, served on the board in 2010-12.

The organization's first major project was to help develop Lilydale Regional Park, located on the Mississippi River across from downtown Saint Paul. Its goal was threefold: to build a significant stone gateway entrance designating the area as a regional park; to build a stone-lined creek along Water Street to catch runoff water from the bluffs to prevent road flooding; and to restore the environment and open views to the river by removing invasive vegetation and planting native plant species. The total project cost was $559,000 and the funds were raised by early 2012.

The third goal was a good fit

Photo: Native trees surround the new stone entry monument to Lilydale Regional Park.

for the Saint Paul Garden Club's conservation and beautification goals. Between 2010 and 2012, the club supported the plant restoration project with three grants totaling $5,000. Funds were earmarked to remove invasive plant species and purchase native plants.

The conservancy aims to be the catalyst for enhancements to Saint Paul's parks. Its second project is to complete restoration of the Oxford Athletic Field, the last piece in a major development of the Oxford Community Center.

Priscilla Brewster

Photo: Tree-covered Water Street leads through Lilydale Regional Park.

Burn Center Patio

at Regions Hospital

In 1998, the Saint Paul Garden Club allocated $3,000 for plantings on the rooftop patio of the Burn Center at Regions Hospital in Saint Paul.

The center, which opened in 1963, is the largest in the Upper Midwest. It treats patients from the surrounding five-state area, often for several months, working through difficult recoveries. The center's designers, Lynn Solem, MD, and Cindy Kuehn, RN, developed the concept of the rooftop garden. Their vision was to provide patients a place to enjoy a garden setting where they could spend time outside with family and friends.

There is a lovely gazebo with wind chimes creating a serene atmosphere. Several benches and tables are surrounded by dozens of planters and decorative objects.

Angel Crandall

Photo: Rooftop garden provides a serene place for patients and guests.

Photo: The garden club toured Swede Hollow Park in Saint Paul in 2010.

Restore, Improve and Protect the Environment Through Conservation, Civic Plantings and Educational Programs

A Profile

Olivia Irvine Dodge, Inspiration and Driving Force

Olivia Irvine Dodge was a distinguished and inspirational member of the Saint Paul Garden Club. She joined in 1967– the year she founded the Thomas Irvine Dodge Nature Center – and continued as a member until her death in 2009.

Inspired by Olivia's vision, the garden club collaborated with three major projects she initiated. As she said during a presentation, "Alone we can do little; together we can do so much."

The first project was her dream of creating a nature center on the property that she and her husband, Arthur, purchased in West Saint Paul. They bought a mansion called Dixie Slopes on 37 acres of land and subsequently acquired 117 more acres for their planned nature center. The nature center opened in 1967. The area now encompasses 320 acres of rolling prairie, meadows, ponds, streams and marshes hidden, somehow, within five square miles of city geography. Over nearly 20 years, the garden club contributed $20,000 to support projects including a prairie garden restoration and a heritage garden.

Showcase for the People

Olivia's plan to reestablish gardens at the Minnesota Governor's Residence was the second project. The English Tudor Revival mansion had been the Irvine's family home. In 1964, after her mother's death, Olivia and her sister, Clotilde Irvine Moles (Mrs. Edwin J., Jr.), donated the home to the state to be the Governor's residence. It was meant to be "the people's house" and a ceremonial showcase. Garden club members raised funds, contributing more than $14,000, and worked "hands on" to recreate lovely gardens through several gubernatorial administrations (see Governor's Residence Garden).

The third project Olivia initiated and the garden club supported with volunteers and funds was the clean-up and improvement of Swede Hollow. An historically significant area of Saint Paul, Swede

Photo: Olivia Irvine Dodge (Mrs. Arthur M.)

Hollow is an 18-acre ravine on the east side of the city that was for many years the neighborhood of the city's immigrant population. The garden club won the Garden Club of America Founders Fund Award in 1977 for turning Swede Hollow from an eyesore into an area in which the entire community could take pride. The club has continued to support rehabilitation of the area, contributing funds totaling more than $64,000 since 1974 (see Swede Hollow Restoration).

Once the garden club completed the initial Swede Hollow project, Olivia would lead new club members on tours of the area, Ellen Fridinger recalled. "She would talk about Swede Hollow and her vision," Ellen said, "and then we would walk around the upper area and down to the lower level."

Father's Influence

Olivia's dreams were the result of her environmental enlightenment. "If you catch people when they are young, I have seen how receptive and appreciative they are about nature. They remember what they learn," she said. Olivia knew this from her own experience. She recalled her father, Horace Hills Irvine, president of Weyerhaeuser Timber Company, taking her on nature walks. "He was very interested in outdoor life and could recognize all the trees and bird calls. These walks along with trips to my grandfather's farm may have been the beginning of my interest in nature," she was quoted as saying.

Olivia was awarded the prestigious Garden Club of America Zone XI Conservation Committee Award in 1988 for her driving role in one of the most successful nature centers in the nation and for outstanding service in the area of conservation.

Olivia won numerous other awards for her many projects and efforts from the state of Minnesota, cities of Saint Paul and Minneapolis, West Saint Paul school district, Minnesota State Horticultural Society and many other organizations. She was praised by Governor Tim Pawlenty as "a woman of vision, generosity and stewardship…an outstanding individual philanthropist". Love, contribution, compassion and generosity were the cornerstones by which she lived. Her passion for life led her to fund a multitude of organizations devoted to protecting the lives of animals and people.

Cathy DeCourcy and Deni Svendsen

Thomas Irvine Dodge Nature Center

The Thomas Irvine Dodge Nature Center was founded by Olivia Irvine Dodge (Mrs. Arthur M.) in 1967– the same year Olivia joined the Saint Paul Garden Club. Olivia, an early leader in environmental education, often spoke about the realization of her dream for an urban nature center in the heart of West Saint Paul.

"With so many areas being developed, it is vitally important that natural areas are saved for future generations.... In this way, children, who learn by doing, will come to appreciate and preserve these natural places....The Nature Center is meant for children from the pre-kindergarten through high school."

The garden club supported the nature center with contributions totaling $20,000 between 1983 and 2010. Funds were used for projects including restoring a prairie garden and creating an heirloom garden. Garden club members Cathy

DeCourcy, Lee Driscoll, Clover Earl and Betty Tiffany served on the board of the nature center and some of them continue the close working relationship.

Olivia's love of her family and grandchildren extended into the community to embrace all the children in the local neighborhoods and public schools. By providing the nature center,

she wanted to teach children her philosophy, which she summarized as:

A love and reverence for the natural world, an appreciation for ecology and conservation, the knowledge that all things are interrelated in nature (what happens to one species carries on to the other species, like a chain), and to become good stewards of the land and to protect natural resources.

Photo: Olivia Dodge and her son, Thomas Irvine Dodge, hike in the nature center.

It was Olivia's hope that a beautiful and serene setting for all to come away from refreshed would instill timeless morals and values that she saw threatened in today's society. It was this commitment that led her to found the nature center, which now encompasses 320 acres and is used by over 40,000 children a year.

Included on site are: A model farm with a maple syrup house, a Family Garden Program, Little Sprouts

Gardening Program, Outdoor Learning Experiences for Garlough School, Dodge Nature Pre-School, summer

camp for children in collaboration with District 197, an after-school science club, hiking trails and Raptor Center and Bird Sanctuary. The center also has a relationship with the Tree Trust, a nonprofit agency employing students and learning-impaired, hearing-impaired and low-income and foster children to do community service projects.

As an elementary school student who benefited from outdoor programs at the Dodge Nature Center, Annie

Svendsen, Deni Svendsen's daughter, referred to Olivia Dodge as "Mother Nature." Her simple mistake was far more appropriate than she understood at the time.

Cathy DeCourcy and Deni Svendsen

Photos, from left: Heirloom garden was created with garden club funds; children learned to propagate plants.

A Profile

Betty Tiffany, A Gracious Leader

Betty Tiffany (Mrs. Francis B.) opened her Sunfish Lake home to Saint Paul Garden Club members on many occasions during her 22 years as an active member. She always greeted us warmly with an engaging smile that seemed to say she was looking forward to all of us having the best time together.

Betty joined the garden club in 1981. She chaired the Horticulture Committee in 1984-85, and served on the committee to reestablish the gardens at the Governor's Residence in Saint Paul from 1986 to 1990. This was a hands-on project by the membership to design and plant new gardens for "the people's house," originally donated to the state by Olivia Irvine Dodge and Clotilde Irvine Moles. Betty worked with Julie Titcomb and Carolyn DeCoster to install an attractive planting in the atrium of the Saint Paul YWCAin 1993. Betty also served as the club's corresponding secretary and vice president, which included serving on the Allocations and Long-Range Planning Committees. She was club president in 1995-96. Betty and Frank added their lively holiday spirits to every Tea Dance, our club's primary fund-raising event.

From 1999 through 2005, Betty chaired the Committee on Swede Hollow. This was a major club project initiated by Olivia Irvine Dodge that has become a signature accomplishment. Betty helped to keep it on the front burner for our membership. New members were taken on fields trips to see the hollow and hear from Olivia. Provisional members, led by Betty, planted native plants on the bluff. Programs were held walking through the hollow for general membership meetings. Betty recruited Cathy DeCourcy and Deni Svendsen to attend neighborhood meetings of residents living near Swede Hollow. They kept the Allocations Committee informed of their need for continuing financial support of the project. The club also funded a sign and plantings at the entrance to the hollow.

Betty and Frank tended their garden, which surrounded their home overlooking Sunfish Lake.

Photo: Betty Tiffany (Mrs. Francis B.)

Frank educated the new arrivals to Sunfish Lake about the scourge of buckthorn and other invasive plants. He taught them how to identify buckthorn and eradicate it from their wooded lots. Frank also promoted good practices for shoreland management and delighted neighbors with maple syrup tapped from the local maple trees. Both he and Betty devoted time and energy to supporting the nearby Dodge Nature Center, which was started by Olivia Irvine Dodge to educate the school children and residents of Saint Paul.

In all her work and accomplishments, Betty's graciousness never failed her. This quality contributed to a sense of community in Sunfish Lake and enhanced productive cooperation within the garden club.

Deni Svendsen and Cathy DeCourcy

Photo, from left: Judy MacManus, Betty Tiffany, Blanche Hawkins and Marla Ordway planted native plants at the Swede Hollow Hamm Mansion site in 2003.

Swede Hollow Restoration
Founders Fund Award Winner

In the 1970s, Olivia Irvine Dodge (Mrs. Arthur M.) and the Saint Paul Garden Club rallied the community to restore an abandoned wooded valley in Saint Paul known as Swede Hollow, which had become a dumping site. The 18-acre valley, located within blocks of Downtown, was an ugly barrier between the city's central business district and one of its closest neighborhoods due to its topography and the rail line running through it. In 1977, the Garden Club of America (GCA) gave our club its coveted Founders Fund award for our restoration efforts.

In the 20 years of Olivia Dodge's involvement, the considerable governmental, financial and neighborhood barriers to the success of this restoration all fell away. Our garden club worked to change the City of Saint Paul's vision for the property from industrial to park land. The

neighboring breweries closed and the Burlington Northern Railroad finally abandoned a line running through the hollow. Since Swede Hollow Park was built in 1995, our club has continued to support the restoration by donating our time in politicking, planting and weeding, and by donating funds to purchase trees, shrubs, rain garden plants and watering devices. Club gifts,

including the Founders Fund award of $6,500, have totaled about $65,000.

Since 2009 our club has also supported the vegetative restoration of a contiguous trail, which runs south from Swede Hollow to where Phalen Creek used to enter the Mississippi River. This area is now known as Bruce Vento Nature Sanctuary (see Tree Legacy Project).

Photo, from left: Garden club volunteers Larry DeLaHunt, Tottie Lilly, Olivia Dodge, Dorothy Fobes and Mimi Davidson

Olivia's original vision was that a pristine Swede Hollow valley would be a link in a trail system that would connect downtown Saint Paul to suburbia, and east to the Minnesota–Wisconsin border. Over 20 years, the project raised funds totaling more than one million dollars from the city, county, state and federal governments, our club, other citizens and companies. Thanks to Olivia's persistence and the work of many, including other members of our club, Olivia's vision is now a reality.

Swede Hollow History

Swede Hollow is located in the valley of Phalen Creek, which runs from Lake Phalen to the Mississippi River. The site where this large river, which bisects our nation, intersects with a small stream is important because it was adjacent to the most northerly flat area on

the river where sternwheelers and steamboats could unload their goods. Because of this geography, a city grew up around this point of commerce and eventually became known as Saint Paul.

In the 1860s a wave of Swedish

immigrants arrived in Saint Paul and found residence in a sheltered hollow that had Phalen Creek running through it. No one in particular appeared to own the land so these newcomers built homes or shanties, according to their skill and funds.

They learned English, found jobs in Saint Paul, sent their children to school and eventually moved up out of the valley and bought or built homes above. Their homes then housed the next groups of immigrants, the Italians, Poles and Mexicans. The city in the 1950s realized that the water the residents were using could be contaminated. The residents were evicted and relocated and their homes were burned.

Swede Hollow then became a dumping ground for garbage, tires, kitchen appliances, old beds and even manufacturers' waste. The highway department considered filling it in for a relocation of Highway 212, and other groups considered filling it to build an industrial park or a tennis club.

Tackling an Eyesore

Whether it was over coffee or

Photo: Swede Hollow, Saint Paul, about 1910

cocktails, there certainly must have been a discussion among the ladies of our garden club that this eyesore known as Swede Hollow could be improved with effort. It was the 1960s and conservation was on the cutting edge, as was the purchase of open space land. The club's idea was to turn Swede Hollow into a nature center park.

Olivia led the effort. In April of 1973, she spoke to her club and to other clubs in GCA's Zone XI. "Conservation is rapidly becoming a growing concern with the garden club as well as with other organizations," she said. "One of the more serious problems facing the United States is the continuing loss of open space land, approximately 7,200 acres every 24 hours. This should be everyone's concern, and each individual should and can do something if only to keep a close eye on his own community and make his voice heard while there is yet time. The Garden Club of America has, in my estimation, a unique opportunity to use its influence and prestige to secure and save for all time some of this invaluable, beautiful, never-to-be-replaced open space land. I, personally, can think of no more exciting project or one

Shows For Swede Hollow

St. Paul Garden Club and Frank Murphy's shop teamed up Wednesday night to present a benefit fashion show of Pauline Trigere's spring collection with proceeds pledged to restoration of Swede Hollow. Swede Hollow is a triangular, eight-acre chunk of land on the East side of St. Paul which has become a dumping ground. Funds from Wednesday's show in St. Paul Hotel will be used to restore the area to its former attractiveness. (For a story about the show, see the People Here & There column, page 15.)

TRIGERE'S superb shaping shows in the aqua-colored gored coat without waistline, above left, worn over a matching skirt worn with printed maillot. Right, a blouson-shaped dress with kimono sleeves for cocktails in the prints that Trigere is fond of for spring.

more worthwhile or with more of a challenge."

In fall 1973, a *Saint Paul Pioneer Press* staff writer, Larry Adcock, produced the following article:

"Swede Hollow Clean-Up Vowed. Saint Paul Mayor Larry Cohen, promising that Swede Hollow would be cleaned up and turned into a park, said, 'We're not just going to be talking about Swede Hollow anymore....You'll start to see something done about it. You've got my commitment....' In the same article Adcock quoted Community Services Director Thomas Kelley, 'Mrs. Arthur Dodge of the city's ladies' garden club had committed to providing funds to install plantings and design a nature center park. Additionally, two neighboring companies, Hamm's Brewing Company and Hoffman Electric Company, have promised to underwrite the massive clean-up project. In the meantime, the city's Public Works Department is issuing violation tags to dumpers and has erected barricades to help prevent further dumping."

Trigere Show Raises Funds

The garden club decided to use the Frank Murphy store and its connections to host a fashion show

Photo: 1974 *Saint Paul Pioneer Press* clipping describing fashion show sponsored by the Frank Murphy store featuring fashions by Pauline Trigere to gain publicity and raise funds for Swede Hollow. The show, held in January 1974, was designed to be an enticing event, with the famous designer Pauline Trigere bringing her fashions and models from New York. Some members of our garden club also modeled the Trigere designs. Frank Murphy's was, at that time, the most fashionable shop in Saint Paul, and vied for that same title in the Twin Cities. Tickets were sold, husbands were invited, cocktails and dinner were served. Olivia presented the garden club's vision for the restoration of Swede Hollow from a dump to a wooded valley park that could be shared by all. The show was a great event, covered by the newspapers. It was successful in raising the awareness of club members' husbands and generated the club's seed money for the project by raising $4,000.

Olivia hoped that Saint Paul's actions would inspire other communities. In her 1974 Bicentennial Project Report on the restoration of Swede Hollow, she wrote, "Every city has its Swede Hollow. Who can better succeed in this exciting undertaking than the member clubs of the Garden Club of America."

In 1974, our club Vice-President, Louise Benz (Mrs. George W.), submitted the proposed Swede Hollow purchase and restoration project to the Founders Fund Committee of the GCA. The GCA selected Swede Hollow as one of three Founders Fund finalists, but our club did not win the award. It wasn't until 1977, after the GCA held its Annual Meeting in Minneapolis, hosted by the Milwaukee Garden Club, our garden club and the Minneapolis-Minnetonka Garden Club (now Lake Minnetonka Garden Club), that we won. It had been a last minute decision to add Swede Hollow to the garden tours. Tour buses loaded with GCA members from all over the nation arrived at the Saint Paul Cathedral and the tour guides, Simpy Fobes, Olivia Dodge, Clover Earl and Alice Weed, boarded their buses and gave the 200 ladies a tour of Swede Hollow and the Dodge Nature Center. Mrs. Dodge hosted the ladies at her Dixie Slope home in West Saint Paul for a delicious luncheon. Delegates encouraged our club to apply again for the Founders Fund, and we did.

Founders Fund at Last

At its 1977 Annual Meeting,

Photo: Olivia Dodge

GCA announced that our club, with support of the Lake Minnetonka Garden Club, Cedar Rapids Garden Club and Garden Club of Denver, had won the Founders Fund Award. There was great rejoicing! The award added $6,500 to the club's coffers for this project.

By then the vision had expanded. There were funds from the city, but also state and federal monies on the horizon. The total budget had increased from thousands to hundreds of thousands. In 1993, Olivia Dodge was finally able to say, "Hallelujah!" The city had received a federal grant of $593,000 to build a trail on the old rail line from the south end of Lake Phalen through Swede Hollow to East Seventh Street. Olivia's original vision was to be actualized. This new purchase and grant would allow for a public pedestrian trail all the way from Stillwater to Lake Phalen to Swede Hollow to East Seventh Street and thence into downtown Saint Paul.

Through many challenges and negotiations over the years, Olivia Dodge and our garden club displayed passion, power and negotiating capabilities. Olivia established a trust fund for Swede Hollow, which produces $9,000 for maintenance

annually. As Olivia passed the baton of Swede Hollow Liaison at our club's annual meeting on July 1, 1997, she said, "I don't think anything next to Dodge Nature Center has given me more challenges or more fulfillment. I thank the garden club for giving me the opportunity to pursue the dream; together we made it a reality."

Native Plant Restoration

With construction completed, other club members took up the baton and interest in native plant restoration sprouted. Initially, Mary Stanley, Betty Tiffany and Alice Weed pursued the native plant concept. The club has since granted funds to the nonprofit Lower Phalen Creek Project to clear invasive buckthorn and honeysuckle, plant trees and shrubs, and restore the park's prairie ecosystem by seeding with native grasses and wildflowers. Project staff has, in turn, worked collaboratively with our club, the Minnesota Community Design Center student teams, the city, Friends of Swede Hollow, the District 4 Community Council and the Minnesota Conservation Corps. What a wonderful collaboration!

A 1997 plan prepared for the Friends of Swede Hollow, "Restoring Lower Phalen Creek, A Strategy for Revitalizing a Neighborhood

Photo: Swede Hollow restored

Ecosystem" by Amy Middleton and Sarah Clark, called for connecting the trail from Swede Hollow Park to Lowertown Saint Paul. This led to the community's response: to plan for what became the Bruce Vento Nature Sanctuary and Bruce Vento Trail System. When visitors leave Swede Hollow through its southern portal, they pass through the 1897 National Architectural Register Helicoidal Railroad Tunnels (built in 1884) and step into the Bruce Vento Nature Sanctuary.

This trail system has continued to be enjoyed by people for walks or nature restoration, and also by both resident and migratory fauna. An annual report on Swede Hollow presented by garden club members Cathy DeCourcy, Deni Svendsen and Betty Tiffany sums up the club's efforts. "A walk down and through the hollow today is an amazingly beautiful sight, with mature plantings, benches, good signage, birds and flowers in abundance. The stream of clear water cascading down the steps of rock, a purifying action, is a delight."

Catherine Nicholson

Tree Legacy Project
Partnership with Bruce Vento Nature Sanctuary

When the Garden Club of America (GCA) asked its member clubs to participate in a Tree Legacy Project for its 2013 Centennial, the Saint Paul Garden Club seized the opportunity to link past environmental achievements with similar commitments to our future.

In 2008, our club decided to initiate a Tree Legacy Project featuring the bur oak, *Quercus macrocarpa*, a valued shade tree native to Minnesota. Led by Mary Gilbertson, the club arranged a partnership within the Bruce Vento Nature Sanctuary in Saint Paul to help restore an oak woodland.

The intention was to build on our club's legacy, dating from the 1970s, of helping transform nearby Swede Hollow into a city nature park (see Swede Hollow). The hollow is located on the city's East Side just north of the nature sanctuary and the two areas are linked by a nature trail. The

sanctuary is located on a sliver of land at the foot of Dayton's Bluff just east of Saint Paul's Lowertown District, with an entry at Commercial Street and East Fourth Street. A century ago the paddle wheelers slowed to land at this northernmost destination on the Mississippi River where a tributary eventually known as Phalen Creek met the great river.

Brownfield Transformed

The 29-acre sanctuary, once an urban brownfield, was opened to the public as a city park in 2005. It is named in honor of Bruce Vento, an avid conservationist, who represented the Saint Paul area in the U.S. Congress from 1977 to 2000. Known as "the environmental conscience of the House of Representatives," Vento

Photo: In 2010, Mary Gilbertson showed garden club members the restored oak woodland they planted in 2009.

was central to passage of more than 300 environmental laws. Restoration of the area took $10 million and a 10-year planning effort involving many neighborhood and civic groups. The U.S. Environmental Protection Agency upgraded soil levels for safe reforestation and understory planting in 2004.

The oak woodland our club helped restore is a group of trees native to the savanna ecosystem of the Mississippi River basin, including bur, red and northern pin oaks, paperback birch, hackberry, pagoda dogwood and sugar maple. The woodland is located near Carver's Cave within the Mississippi River flyway. The cave is the original *wakan tipi* (spirit house) known to the Dakota as a sacred and mysterious place. By helping restore the woodland, our club hopes to expand migratory bird habitat in the flyway.

In April 2009, garden club members planted saplings and forbs at one of the last planned areas of oak woodland restoration within the nature sanctuary. Our volunteers worked with students from science classes at Mounds Park Academy,

U.S. Park Rangers, and crews from the Saint Paul Parks and Recreation Department. We provided tree guards and fencing to protect the 220 new trees via a $1,000 grant to the Lower Phalen Creek Project. This is a citizens' group that has spearheaded ecological restoration work in the nature sanctuary.

In June 2010, garden club members embarked on a caravan tour of Swede Hollow and the Bruce Vento Nature Sanctuary. They returned to the oak woodland and checked growth of the saplings, then 14 months in the ground and thriving. The area charmed us all, so close to Downtown yet so natural, with birdsong floating overhead and on the nearby pond. We continued to support the restoration in 2012 and 2013 by granting $3,225 to buy plants for the greenway between the hollow and the nature sanctuary, and to plant trees and native grasses at the entryway to the sanctuary.

Acorns Propagated

Members continued our tree project by collecting species acorns, propagating them, and nurturing oak seedlings. In June 2011, members and a city natural resource staffer

Photos, from left; Mounds Park Academy students helped plant trees; and bur oak and white oak seedlings at our 2012 flower show.

planted the seedlings on a hillside in the nature sanctuary, and then photographed and documented the plantings. About half of our seedlings survived the subsequent drought, Mary reported.

Challenge Class in propagating acorns to our garden club's "The Way We Were" flower show at the Minnesota History Center. Members exhibited one- and two-year bur oak and white oak seedlings. Mary Gilbertson won

The club has built on its core tree legacy project by creating two spin-off projects. In 2009 and 2010, our Allocations Committee encouraged grant applicants to propose tree-planting projects—and they did. In 2012, we added a Horticulture

the Novice Award in Horticulture from the Garden Club of America for her first-place exhibit, and our club won a GCA Commendation for the overall exhibit.

Mary Gilbertson

Photo, from left: In the lead on a garden club stroll through the Bruce Vento Sanctuary in 2010 were Nancy Scherer, Shari Wilsey, Colleen FitzPatrick, Maureen Adelman, Joan Duddingston and Mary Dennis.

Freshwater Society

Protecting Water Resources

The Saint Paul Garden Club supported the work of the Freshwater Society annually from 1978 through 1999, contributing a total of $4,625 to this nonprofit organization. The society is dedicated to educating and inspiring people to value, conserve and protect all freshwater resources.

Our club's most significant contributions were made in 1984 and 1987. The first funded a Teacher's Guide for a film about the Mississippi River. The second helped to create curriculum for a Weather/Environment Calendar. This popular calendar is one of the society's best known projects.

The society also publishes a quarterly newsletter for friends and members and other brochures informing the public about its initiatives, such as the "Community Cleanup for Water Quality" and "Things YOU Can Do to Protect Water." Currently, the society has launched a "Work for Water" campaign, offering several sponsorship opportunities.

The garden club's contributions to the Freshwater Society are an indication of our dedication and commitment to support valuable community organizations in their efforts to protect and preserve our environment and natural resources.

Mollie Keys

Great River Greening
Reforesting the River Valley

What was to become a Saint Paul Garden Club long-term environmental endeavor to improve the Mississippi River began in October 1990. A conservation report was issued to our club from Marilyn Magid, conservation representative of Zone XI of the Garden Club of America (GCA). She invited other GCA Zones (V, VII, IX and X) to join with our Zone XI in advocating for the cleanup of the Mississippi and its drainage areas.

Marilyn's report documented the importance of the river as an ecosystem and the compromised condition of the river. It said the Mississippi, 2,368 miles long, contains drainage from 31 states. The water quality and the land adjoining the river had been affected by the pesticides, herbicides, solvents and trace minerals discharged into the river by factories, farms and sewers. The uppermost regions of the river

were the least polluted, with farm runoff the chief polluter. In the Minneapolis-Saint Paul area, industrial pollution entered the Mississippi in a more significant volume.

The GCA Conservation Committee and Executive Committee approved a statement that the GCA supports a policy to endorse a reasonable restoration and

maintenance of the water quality and ecological integrity of the Mississippi River system.

In 1992, nationally known architect Ben Thompson, a Saint Paul native, provided his vision for a community-based organization to restore prairies, forests and waters of the local area. He painted two pictures of what he called "Great River Park"–

Photo: Club members planted trees along the Mississippi River in 2008 (see page 102 for names).

showing views of Saint Paul and the Mississippi from Mounds Park in summer and winter—which captured the imagination of civic leaders. In fall 1993, the Saint Paul Foundation funded the preparation of a white paper for incoming Mayor Norm Coleman to provide a status report of riverfront development and issues. The report recommended reforestation along the river bluffs in downtown Saint Paul to restore ecological function and create attractive green spaces. The Saint Paul Riverfront Corporation agreed to fund work to explore how citizens could be involved in planting efforts. The project was renamed "Greening Great River Park."

Conservation Exhibit a Winner

Our garden club recognized this opportunity to help fulfill GCA's Mississippi River restoration pledge and, over the next 18 years, provided grants, public education and hands-

on planting. The club made its first donation, $2,000, in 1994, when President Lucy Dunning wrote a letter to Mayor Coleman expressing the club's interest in the greening project and offering our help.

A conservation exhibit, "The Greening of Saint Paul: Restoring

Our Natural Heritage," was presented by our conservation chairs, Ellen Fridinger and Colles Larkin, at our club's GCA Small Flower Show at the Town and Country Club in Saint Paul in September, 1995. The exhibit focused on efforts of Saint Paulites

to maintain and enlarge the city's green spaces over the course of 100 years. A map presenting the goals of the greening project was presented as well as a case study of the Design Center for American Urban Landscape indicating the city's future direction. The GCA Marion Thompson-Fuller Brown Conservation Award was presented to Ellen and Colles for their exhibit. The award recognized the exhibit as one of exceptional educational and visual merit, which increased the public's knowledge and awareness of the environment.

Support for Reforesting

In 1997, the garden club gave $7,500 to the greening reforestation project, which was funded mainly with large state grants. By the end of the year, 24,100 trees and shrubs had been added to the river valley through the efforts of 5,000 volunteers, including members of our club.

Between 2005 and 2011, the club gave five grants totaling $11,200 to the project, which had been renamed

Photo: Colles Larkin and Ellen Fridinger with their award-winning exhibit

"Great River Greening" in 1999. The first grant helped purchase seed and plants to improve the ecological function and aesthetic quality of the storm water basin. Volunteers helped remove acres of invasive species.

On Arbor Day, April 27, 2007, the garden club received a prestigious award from Great River Greening. The citation reads, "The Saint Paul Garden Club, because of its commitment to urban beautification as demonstrated by its enduring relationship with Rice Park, its role with Blooming Saint Paul, its reintroduction of Swede Hollow to the Saint Paul community, and its commitment to conservation and land stewardship through its significant support of Great River Greening, has been chosen as the Non-Profit Environmental Steward of the Year." Club President Ellen Bruner accepted the award.

As a part of a Million Dollar Campaign in 2007, the greening project partnered with the state Department of Natural Resources and Saint Croix Watershed Research Station to direct a large hardwood seeding effort. The garden club

donated spring planting materials to help improve and enlarge the habitat for Minnesota's bird species "of greatest conservation need." In 2008, the club donated funds to restore the oak savannah in Indian Mounds Park and in 2009 to restore the oak savannah at the Westside Blufflands.

By the end of 2010, 25,629 volunteers from the community and garden club had planted 60,586 trees and shrubs and had restored 40,000 acres of land along the Mississippi River.

Deb Venker

Club volunteers, from page 100:
From left: Carol Kolb, Colles Larkin, Christine Umhoefer, Sharon Prokosch, Bonnie Hollibush, Ellen Maas Pratt, Paula Soholt, Pam Nuffort, Judy MacManus, Ingrid Conant and Maureen Adelman.

Photo, from left: Charlotte Drake and Mary Stanley helped plant seedling trees along the Mississippi River.

Highway Billboards Protest

Marching to State Capitol

The proliferation of highway billboards that blighted the landscape of Minnesota and the entire country in the 1950s and early 1960s spurred the Saint Paul Garden Club to action. Led by the Conservation Committee, members worked to educate citizens and lobbied against the billboards.

Garden club members became activists in the cause of eliminating "litter on a stick." They sent letters and telegrams to President Dwight D. Eisenhower as well as to Minnesota congressmen, as reported by Betty Slade (Mrs. G. Norman), conservation chairman, in the committee's annual report for 1957-58.

During the 1958-59 year, members Annetta Morgan (Mrs. John) and Gerry Thompson (Mrs. Horace) were noted for spending much effort on the issue and meeting with the Minnesota Highway Commissioner. In 1960, garden club members marched to the State Capitol to protest the installation of new billboards along Minnesota highways.

Five years later, the Highway Beautification Act of 1965, proposed by President Lyndon Baines Johnson and supported by his wife, Claudia "Lady Bird" Johnson, was passed. The law called for control of outdoor advertising. It required states to regulate outdoor ads along the Federal Interstate Highway System and the Federal-Aid Primary Highway System in order to receive full federal highway funding. The penalty for noncompliance was loss of 10 percent of those funds.

The Minnesota Legislature complied with the federal law in 1971 by passing the Minnesota Outdoor Advertising Act, limiting billboards along federal highways to areas zoned for business and industrial activities.

Deb Venker

Katherine Abbott Girl Scout Camp
Planting for the Future

In the 1950s, the Saint Paul Garden Club supported a new Girl Scout Camp in Mahtomedi by planting trees and shrubs on the grounds. Although the camp was converted to a city park in the 1980s, those trees are still thriving more than 50 years later!

The camp, located on a 72-acre plot of hardwood forest, prairie and wetlands, was the inspiration of Miss Katherine Abbott, the daughter of a prominent Saint Paul physician. An active adult Girl Scout volunteer, she dreamed of creating a troop camp that would be easily accessible to area Girl Scouts. She died on Oct. 3, 1946, before her dream could be realized, but many friends worked in her memory to create the camp just a few years later. The first parcel, located southeast of White Bear Lake, was purchased in 1950. In 1952, the Girl Scout Camp was officially opened and dedicated to the memory of Katherine Abbott.

Contributions for the camp came from the Katherine Abbott Memorial Fund. Additional philanthropic support from members of the Saint Paul community, some of whom were involved with the Saint Paul Garden Club, made completion of the camp possible. A streetcar operated by the Minneapolis and Saint Paul Suburban Railroad Company took girls from downtown Saint Paul directly to the front gate of the camp along Lincolntown Avenue.

Club Plans Planting Project

The garden club became aware of a need for plantings on the camp grounds. The "adoption of the Girl Scout Camp planting project" is noted in President Elizabeth (Betty) Slade's Report of 1953-54. A Conservation Committee meeting was held at the

104

Photo: A crabapple tree provides climbing fun for Susan Brust's Girl Scout Troop 2251, including Susan's daughter, Kelsie (left), in 1999.

camp in September, 1954. Members had a picnic in the Camp House and heard a talk on trees by Dr. Gustav Hard of the Horticultural Department at the University of Minnesota. They also heard from the district director and advisor for the camp, who told them that 1,600 to 2,000 girls had visited the camp that summer.

In 1954, the garden club gave $402.45 for the planting project at the camp. A report from Vice-President Annetta Morgan dated 1954-55 states that along with the chairpersons of the Conservation Committee, Anne White, and Horticultural Committee, Charlotte Ordway, the garden club successfully carried out the first part of the project.

In May, 1955, Betty and Annetta met at Girl Scout Headquarters to discuss future plans. That spring, the club planted two Hoffa crabapple trees and transplanted 20 Norway (red) pines from the garden of a club member. Many of the trees were planted around the camp flag pole to create a future backdrop for the Girl Scouts' flag ceremonies. Due to a severe drought that spring and severe summer heat, many of the pines did not survive. Anne and Charlotte contributed $15 and the club planted 11 more pines in August.

Lilacs Thrived

In spring 1956, 15 Norway pine seedlings were planted and several lilac shoots transplanted at the camp. The following spring, "The Norway pines may not have done so well, but the transplanted lilacs were thriving," according to a Conservation Committee report.

The City of Mahtomedi acquired the camp from the Girl Scout Council in the 1980s and now maintains the building and property as the lovely and popular Katherine Abbott Park. The original flag pole no longer stands, but its concrete base with the remains of a wooden pole in the center can be found in front of a stately stand of Norway pines beyond the east end of the parking lot. The trees may have struggled, but they are thriving now. Some lilac bushes and crab trees are there, too. Their blossoms are a sight to behold in the spring thanks to garden club members who had the foresight and generosity to plant them so many years ago.

Kim Ozzello and Susan Brust

Student Conservation Association
Building Future Leaders

The Saint Paul Garden Club has a long history of supporting the Student Conservation Association. The association is well aligned with our club goals, with a mission "to build the next generation of conservation leaders and inspire stewardship of our environment and communities by engaging young people in hands-on service to the land."

A 1955 *Harper's Magazine* article titled "Let's Close our National Parks" stated that under-resourced parks should be shut down for their own good because they were being "loved to death." Vassar College student Elizabeth Cushman wrote a response to this article for her senior thesis and, from this, the association was soon born.

Student members of all ages work to protect and restore national parks, marine sanctuaries, cultural landmarks and community green spaces in all 50 states and throughout the world.

The association provides year-round training and service opportunities to high school and college students with hands-on programs that range from tracking grizzlies through the Tetons, to restoring desert ecosystems, to teaching environmental education at Washington D.C.'s Urban Tree House.

Our club's support for the association began with a $100 donation in 1973 when Alice Weed (Mrs. George) was president and Elisabeth Ljungkull (Mrs. Rolf) was treasurer. The club contributed $2,900 to the association from 1973 to 2004 from its Community Fund.

Susan Brust and Kim Ozzello

Holcombe Circle Association

Introducing Children to Nature

School-based community gardens were a novel concept in 1989 when the Saint Paul Garden Club was approached about funding a garden in the courtyard of an inner-city elementary school in Saint Paul. The project, proposed by the Holcombe Circle Association, introduced the study of horticulture to children in preschool and elementary grades at Maxfield Elementary School on Victoria Street North.

The project was dedicated to "making the neighborhood nicer," recalled Twinks Irvine, who sponsored the request. The garden club provided $250 for river birch, arborvitae, and Miss Kim lilacs, which were planted and maintained by school and association members.

The Maxfield School courtyard was one of several neighborhood projects the garden club funded

between 1987 and 2001 at the request of Earlene Johnson, Holcombe Circle Association president. Our club granted funds totaling $1,885. One project provided shrubs and nature books so preschool children at the Head Start facility on Fuller Ave., could develop relationships with nature. Another was to improve gardens on the (former) Amherst H.

Wilder Foundation Campus on Lafond Ave.

Carolynn Lund

Photo: Holcombe Circle Park in Saint Paul's Summit-University neighborhood

O.H. Anderson School Trail
An outdoor Classroom

Seven grants to help create an outdoor environmental classroom for the students of O.H. Anderson Elementary School in Mahtomedi were made by the Saint Paul Garden Club between 2000 and 2007. The grants, requested by the school's Nature Trail Committee, totaled $7,565. Garden club member Ellie Bruner sponsored the requests.

Funds were used to restore a native prairie and a meadow behind the school. A nature trail, created in 1982, runs through this area. The restored area offers twelve environmental learning stations, including science, social studies, language art, math, physical education and the arts.

Several steps were taken to prepare the land, including eradication of non-native plants and soil preparation to grow prairie plants and grasses. Students planted native plants with support from a professional prairie

restoration business and Great River Greening.

Today, diverse wildlife is attracted to the land, adding further to its educational value. Teachers and students often make use of the area, which has been integrated into the school's curriculum. That integration extends to after-school and summer programs, maximizing the benefit of this special learning space.

Angel Crandall

Photo: O.H. Anderson School trail

Somerset School Butterfly Garden

Engaging a School Community

A butterfly garden of wildflowers can provide a welcoming habitat for our fluttery friends and beautify the surrounding area. It also can engage an entire school community in a rewarding project.

That's what happened in 2010, when the Saint Paul Garden Club gave Somerset Elementary School in Mendota Heights $500 to create a butterfly garden on an unused part of the school playground. The Somerset PTA contributed, too. The school proposed to plan, build and plant the garden, involving all the students in its pre-kindergarten through grade four classes. The proposal was sponsored by garden club member Ingrid Conant.

A teacher sketched an artist's vision of a winding path with beds of wildflowers and a member of the Somerset Garden Club designed the beds. In the spring, grounds staff helped clear the land and cut logs into

garden seats and a table. One family donated boulders from its property while other parents defined planting beds. Cub Scouts helped mulch a pathway and prepared the soil for planting. Another group bought 400 seedling wildflowers.

June 4 was declared "planting day" and everyone in the school participated. One boy who had

started milkweed plants from seed in an after-school class planted the seedlings. In the fall, the new kindergartners planted daffodil bulbs. Many of the plants, which included purple coneflower, blanket flower and butterfly weed, bloomed the first year, attracting both butterflies and bees.

Mary Dennis

Photo: Students planted flowers to attract butterflies.

Expo Elementary School Garden
Growing an Interest in Plants

What does a school program interested in gardening do with $2,700 from the Saint Paul Garden Club?

From 1991 to 1994, Expo Elementary School students in kindergarten through grade five used our funding to plant a flower and vegetable garden on a 2,000 square-foot plot on the school grounds in the Macalester-Groveland neighborhood of Saint Paul. Then, they created a Peace Garden, a sunflower house, a bean tunnel and an herb garden.

The garden was part of a year-long environmental curriculum called Earth Care. Expo's students learned about organic gardening, pest management, energy conservation, planting to attract wildlife and "cityscaping." The school also used part of our club's donation to buy Growlabs light tables so students could start plants indoors and grow plants during the winter. The Growlabs were used successfully for

several years.

Kristi Tschida, the after-school childcare director in charge of the gardening project, reported on the school garden: "It was wonderful, but lack of a water source and vandalism were the biggest road blocks back then. We would build a bean hut and the next day it would be torn down or burned down. Even after we stopped

gardening it was like a little forest – which was a great place to play and learn – but when it became a teen hangout we lost most of it. The school district had to cut it down."

Nancy Scherer

Photo: Expo Elementary School kids clowned in their flower garden.

Eco Education
Stewardship in Action

A random sample of 1,000 adult Minnesotans surveyed to determine their "environmental literacy" was conducted by the Minnesota Report Card on Environmental Literacy in 2004. Among all age groups, adults 18 to 34 scored near the bottom on knowledge regarding the environment. This significant and troubling finding pointed to the need for environmental education in our schools. Eco Education, a nonprofit organization based in Saint Paul, is addressing this need.

The Saint Paul Garden Club supported Eco Education from 1996 to 2009 with grants totaling $3,800. The organization promotes environmental learning and empowering our young people to become actively involved while learning. It serves as a bridge connecting schools with the community.

Each year more than 1,000

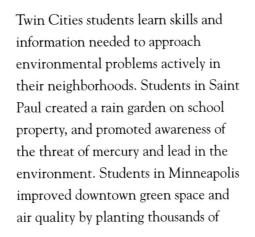

Twin Cities students learn skills and information needed to approach environmental problems actively in their neighborhoods. Students in Saint Paul created a rain garden on school property, and promoted awareness of the threat of mercury and lead in the environment. Students in Minneapolis improved downtown green space and air quality by planting thousands of

flowers at Peavy Plaza and Loring Greenway. Students learn by doing and see that their efforts can make a positive change.

To help teachers, Eco Education offers professional development in environmental education service-learning and community problem solving.

Deni Svendsen

Photo: Projects encourage students to become environmental stewards in their neighborhoods.

Photo: Marge Hols' English cottage garden was among club members' gardens toured during the 2003 Garden Club of America Zone XI meeting in Saint Paul.

Share the Advantages of Association Via
Meetings, Conferences, Correspondence
and Publications

Horticulture
A Passion for Plants

Drawn together by our love of gardening, members of the Saint Paul Garden Club have explored many aspects of horticulture – the science and art of growing flowers, ornamental plants, fruits and vegetables. For eighty years, the club's Plant & Seed and Horticulture Committees have nurtured our passion for plants. A sampling of these adventures follows.

"Two members grew the perennial forget-me-not, *Cynoglossum nervosum,* sent from the New York Botanical Garden," Charlotte Ordway, horticulture chairman, reported in 1955. "The seeds from the first bloom were sown and we have several plants for next year. We hope it will winter successfully as it is a beautiful shade of royal blue."

In 1958, club members' "increasing interest in growing dahlias" led to a talk by a member of the Minnesota Dahlia Society. "In September we

had an informal dahlia show and the Garden Club of America (GCA) horticulture award was presented to Mary Alexander," horticulture chairman Annetta Morgan reported. As suggested by GCA, the club chose ornamental crabapples as its future horticultural specialty. "The following year we planted flowering crab trees at the Children's Hospital," wrote

horticulture chairman Alice Weed.

Lady's Slippers at the Gov's

"Alice Harrison and her committee prepared a new section of ground for a wildflower garden at the Governor's Residence on Summit Avenue," Glenna Price wrote in 1978. "…Our state flower, the showy lady's slipper, will be planted in this area. The wildflower garden looks lovely

Photo: Garden club members toured Alice Harrison's peaceful Japanese garden in Sunfish Lake in July 1994.

in the spring and our plants are doing nicely." In 1979 Miriam Messing noted, "The showy lady's slippers came up in the spring and produced a lovely mass of color."

The club's desire to make a good showing at the Plant Exchange during GCA annual meetings was emphasized by many horticulture chairmen over the years. For each PX, the GCA issued a challenge – usually to exhibit six plants propagated from seed or cuttings. Club delegates brought home plants exhibited by other clubs, and many of these treasures still grow in our gardens.

"Our contribution to the Plant Exchange this year was round-lobed hepatica," Glenna Price reported in 1978. "Next year it will be field thistle in connection with the Compositae Family, which our zone is studying. GCA is having each zone study a plant family and each club a plant in that family. We hopefully will know all about field thistles. Each member will be trying to grow them this winter. I pray we are successful; if not, we've had it."

"Presently we are parceling out seeds and cuttings to various members to try to produce 'Something for the Birds' for the GCA Plant Exchange. I sincerely hope the results won't be 'for the birds'," Miriam Messing commented in 1979.

Through the 1980s, horticulture chairmen reported on attempts to propagate trees and shrubs from cuttings, often with disappointing results. In 1980-81, the Horticulture Committee arranged workshops at the University of Minnesota Horticultural Research Center "to develop members' interest and skill in plant propagation from hardwood and softwood cuttings, and to propagate healthy plant specimens to take to the GCA Plant Exchange in Cincinnati in 1981." Alas, only Alma Derauf, who had a greenhouse, succeeded in propagating cuttings of red-osier dogwood and winning two merit awards at the PX. "We want to go on record as saying plant propagation from softwood and hardwood cuttings isn't easy in Minnesota," Georgia DeCoster reported. The following year four members produced plants for the PX and Tottie Lilly won an award for a Kentucky coffeetree grown from seed.

A Minnesota Garden Diary, a small loose-leaf notebook, was compiled by the garden club in 1983, with Elisabeth Ljungkull, known as Peter, as editor. Chapters described what to do each season as well as how to grow lilies, orchids and roses. "Our

Photo, from left: Tottie Lilly, Shannon Pulver, Jeanne Felder and Ann McMillan chose plants for the GCA Plant Exchange in 2004.

diary begins with September for two reasons," Peter wrote. "January isn't a beginning for anything. And, if you didn't start it in September, you won't enjoy it in May."

The club donated funds "to ensure the preservation, propagation and dissemination of the prairie white-fringed orchid, *Platanthera leucophea,* an endangered native Minnesota wildflower." Horticulture chair Joan Duddingston noted in 1991 that the club completed its pledge of $5,000 to the National Center for Plant Conservation.

Fearless Fern Growers

A multi-year study of ferns began in 1993, when landscape architect and university professor Dr. C. Colston Burrell gave an illustrated lecture on the reproduction cycle of fern spores. Charlotte Drake, horticulture chair, reported that Cole brought ten different kinds of fern spores and taught a hands-on workshop. Members started fern spores in clear plastic sweater boxes for the 1994 GCA Zone XI Plant Exchange in Milwaukee. "Our effort to propagate ferns from spores has been a long and delicate effort with some failure and only moderate success," horticulture chair Jeanne Felder wrote in 1994. "…We do not have what could be called robust ferns. The "fearless fern growers" persevered, however, and all six of the plants they took to Milwaukee won merit awards, according to Mimi (Priscilla) Brewster, 1994-95 horticulture chair.

"Hydroponics by Our Own SPGC Horticulture Committee" read the notice for our club's April 1996 meeting. Following two workshops taught by Charlotte Drake on growing vegetables hydroponically, "We covered three large tables with overflowing plants to show the other members our accomplishments," reported Shannon Murphy Pulver. "We then washed, tossed [and served] the salad, which was absolutely delicious."

Workshops since the late 1990s have run the gamut: We've grown bur and white oak seedlings from acorns and started native plants in plastic jugs by the winter sowing method. We've propagated African

Photos, from left: Charlotte Drake, Pam Attia, Ingrid Conant and Priscilla Brewster with their entry for the Milwaukee "Art en Fleurs" Show in 2001; and Catherine Nicholson with water gardening expert Soni Forsman in 2006

violets and rhizomatous begonias from leaf cuttings. We've trained scented geranium topiary standards and created container water gardens. We've made troughs for tiny Alpine perennials and constructed living wreaths from moss and small succulents. Ruth

Huss tutored us on orchids. Dorothy Reed taught us which flowers to grow for dried arrangements. Sally Brown guided us in making garden stepping stones embellished with designs and glitter.

Several club members have provided horticultural leadership beyond our own club. Charlotte

Drake, Mary Stanley and Priscilla Brewster served terms as GCA Zone XI horticulture chairs. They also served as GCA horticulture judges, traveling to GCA flower shows around the country. Carol Kolb is currently a horticulture judge.

Field trips continue to inspire us. To create herbarium specimens for our 2012 flower show, we arranged a workshop at the Bell Museum Herbarium on the University of Minnesota Saint Paul Campus. Members harvested, dried and mounted perennials and ferns, and entered 18 artistic specimens in the show.

Gathering ideas from each other's gardens has long been a favorite summer activity. We've toured our members' gardens in Dellwood, Mahtomedi, Saint Paul, Stillwater and Sunfish Lake.

Through it all, we're tried–again and again–to master the botanical names for our plants, which are required for flower show entries.

Mary Stanley invented little games and quizzes to entice us to learn the

nomenclature. Colleen FitzPatrick wrote and starred in a skit to enlighten us. Nancy Scherer offered "Latin Lite" and "Latin Heavy" slideshow presentations in living color. Alas, most of us still would earn no more than a "Gentlewoman's C".

Marge Hols

Photos, from left: Mrs. Horace Klein with her hort entry in 1936; and Marilee Elsholtz in her spectactular Dellwood garden

Conservation
Education and Activism

As a new member of the Garden Club of America (GCA) in the 1930s, the Saint Paul Garden Club was encouraged to look beyond members' gardens to the bigger picture: conservation of the environment.

By 1940, our club had established a Conservation Committee independent of its Horticulture Committee. The new committee focused on educating our members and others in the community about conservation.

In 1954, we gave scholarships to grade school teachers for two-week sessions at an Audubon Camp in Wisconsin to develop programs in conservation and natural history. The teachers created *The World Around You*, an introductory pamphlet for use in schools. When the GCA National Committee on Conservation requested slides of Minnesota wildflowers, the club responded by sending eight

beautiful slides of wild orchids given by Mr. John Briggs. As early as 1955 the club studied plants to attract birds and the interaction of plants and animals. We also began an "Anti-Litterbug Campaign" to foster an awareness of the need to clean up the environment.

A "Keep America Beautiful" campaign was stressed at the GCA Zone XI Meeting hosted by our club

in 1956. Early activism started as club members contacted state and federal legislators and even wrote President Eisenhower urging action to control the proliferation of billboards along state and federal highways (see Highway Billboards Protest). According to Elizabeth Slade, conservation chairman, "...Mrs. John Morgan's article, '41,000 Miles of New

Photo: Dodge Nature Center prairie planting

118

Highways', was printed in the April issue of *The Minnesota Horticulturist*. In response, Mrs. Morgan was invited to speak at a meeting of the Men's Garden Club of White Bear Lake. Could anything be more triumphant?"

Our members' growing awareness of their environment was prophetic. Another topic at the 1957 Zone

Meeting was the declining bird population and a suspected connection to the use of insecticides, particularly those used to control mosquitoes. Predating Rachel Carson's 1961 book, *Silent Spring*, Conservation Committee members held a roundtable discussion of their observations on this issue. Mrs. Slade advised them to write to their legislators.

The 1960s was a decade of collaboration on three major conservation projects. Our club members' efforts and contributions helped create the Minnesota Landscape Arboretum. Inspired by club member Olivia Dodge, a forward thinking conservationist, we also helped establish the Dodge Nature Center and Swede Hollow Park. Our club has continued to support these community treasures through the years.

In 1975, the club studied the growing blight of Dutch elm disease and oak wilt that was destroying much of the graceful tree canopy along our neighborhood streets. Speakers informed our members, who then distributed pamphlets to neighbors and friends. Our environmental concerns reached beyond the Twin Cities: A member of the Sierra Club spoke to us about the effects of copper/nickel mining in the Boundary Waters Canoe Area.

Recycling Unlimited

When "Reduce, Reuse, Recycle" became a catch phrase in the 1970s, Helen Lindeke, Lee Driscoll and Clover Earl responded. They advocated promoting the growth and development of Recycling Unlimited (R.U.), a small operation that served some Saint Paul residents. They studied the city's solid waste disposal situation and "met with the corporate world head on." They even took their cause to the Metropolitan Council. Committee members wrote a grant proposal and obtained support for R.U. of $3,000 each from a garden club member and the Saint Paul Companies. According to notes by Clover Earl, "Helen and I, needless to say, have true faith in R. U. and its potential. We are committed to the need to address immediately the problem of solid waste by means of recycling." R.U. paved the way for Saint Paul's current citywide curbside

Photo: Elizabeth (Betty) Slade (Mrs. G. Norman)

recycling program.

Other environmental concerns caught our attention. A speaker from the Minnesota Pollution Control Agency informed the club about acid rain and its impact on the ecosystem. We were also alerted to the problem of purple loosestrife, a popular perennial that had escaped our gardens and was encroaching on our wetlands and lake shores.

Lucy Dunning, conservation chair 1989-90, encouraged our members to learn about the Congressional agenda and to contact our senators and congressmen. She provided phone numbers and noted that "all three offices (Sen. Boschwitz, Sen. Durenberger and Rep. Vento) were eager to hear how constituents wanted them to vote on specific bills."

In 1990–91, Helen Comfort, conservation chair, wrote of club

President Mary Stanley, "And Mary said, 'Let there be fun for the club with the Conservation Committee.' Field trips were born." In the fall, we took trips to see Schaefer Prairie in bloom, Dennison Area to hunt for prairie bush clover and rare plants, Dodge Nature Center for education

and a prairie tour; and Wolsfeld Woods to see a big woods remnant. In the spring, we toured the Pig's Eye sewage treatment plant and Northern States Power yard waste composting facility. For even more fun, we hiked in the River Bend Nature Center Wildflower Walk, which featured colonies of the rare dwarf trout lily in bloom.

Catherine Goes to Washington

Catherine Nicholson, a new member and former Minnesota Pollution Control Agency employee, attended a meeting of the GCA Conservation and National Affairs and Legislation Committee in 1991. She learned about national environmental issues from GCA position papers and called on the Minnesota Congressional Delegation. In 1993, Catherine returned to the GCA meeting with President Lucy Dunning. Over the years, Catherine and other club members continued to attend and our efforts were not in vain. The GCA legislative consultant credited

Photo: Field trip to Ingrid Conant's Lime Springs, Iowa farm and Hayden Prairie in 1998 (see page 122 for names).

Catherine and our club in persuading Minnesota's Republican senator to provide the swing vote that allowed for protection of the Arctic National Wildlife Refuge (ANWAR) in 2006.

As conservation chair in 1998-99, Catherine, eager to show the club where all their garbage went, took members to different types of solid waste sites: the BFI Pine Bend landfill, the adjacent BFI "Recyclery" and the SKB co-compost facility, which composted yard waste and food waste from institutions. Members saw the SKB Demolition Landfill, where the goal was to find reuses for construction waste rather than put it in landfills.

A field trip to Eco Education, one of the club's funded agencies, introduced members to worm composting. We saw a video presentation and were instructed on how to build our own composters for home use. Each member received one pound of compost worms and fed the worms newspaper and vegetable scraps. The goal was to reduce the amount of waste generated and to develop some good compost in our homes over the winter. Success was varied as some of the worms were "thinking outside the box."

In January 1999, our entire membership visited the Minnesota State Capitol. Republican senators, Democratic representatives and Minnesota Pollution Control Agency members spoke to us. We learned about the inner workings of environmental policies and politics at the State Capitol. However, as noted by Catherine, "Probably the most amazing was the visit with our brand new Governor, Jesse Ventura. He learned about our club and told us of his roots in politics stemming from a wetland issue." As a member present, Deni Svendsen was struck by the two apparent bodyguards flanking the impressively sized governor. He was well protected for his meeting with the Saint Paul Garden Club.

Big Picture Grows Bigger

The 2000s heralded new information that engaged our conservation chairs: Mary Stanley, Mary Dennis, Roddie Turner, Colles Larkin, Pegi Harkness, Andrea McCue, Blanche Hawkins and Kate Booth. They invited speakers to help us understand the interaction of environmental systems. They also emphasized the importance of conservation and national affairs.

Photo, from left: Sally Brown, her mother Diane Roth and Betty Cammack donned hardhats for a Pig's Eye Sewage Treatment Plant tour in the early 1990s.

Colles assumed regional and national leadership positions, first as Zone XI representative to the GCA Conservation Committee and the National Affairs and Legislation Committee in 2007-09. She then served on the GCA Conservation Committee as vice chair for agriculture in 2009-11.

Our club was introduced to the Nature Conservancy, and heard programs on prairie restoration and the preservation of plant species. We visited the Cedar Creek Natural History Area, a junction of western prairie, northern boreal forest and the big woods deciduous forest. We got updates on Mississippi riverfront development and viewed a film called "Troubled Waters: A Mississippi River Story." We learned about flowers of the past, backyard

birds, bees, rain gardens and rain forest conservation.

A presentation in 2005 on "Global Warming and Climate Change in Minnesota: An Introduction to Minnesota's Scientific and Natural Areas" elevated our concern for this ominous issue. Paul Red Elk, a consultant at Gibbs Farm, fascinated us with a talk on "Preservation of American Indian Agriculture."

The garden club continues its dedication to conservation by supporting the work of local conservation groups and programs for children in schools with grants from our Community Fund. Our political activism continues as our Conservation Committee keeps us abreast of environmental issues and upcoming legislation and encourages us to contact our legislators.

Deni Svendsen

Members on field trip, from page 120:
From left front: Mary Dennis, Carol Kolb, Hella Hueg, Ellen Fridinger, Tottie Lilly, Ann McMillan, Deni Svendsen, Nancy Martin, Betty Cammack; back: Ingrid Conant, Julie Titcomb, Elise Tesar, Catherine Nicholson and Faye Duvall

Photo, from left: Colleen FitzPatrick, Vicky Holman, Sue Zechmann, Blanche Hawkins, Angel Crandall and Colleen Hooley toured Cloverdale Farm in 2008.

Photography
A New Adventure

The Saint Paul Garden Club ventured into photography in June 2003, when we included a photography division in the flower show at the Garden Club of America (GCA) Zone XI Meeting in Saint Paul. At that time, only a few GCA garden clubs had held photography shows.

"There were no rules or regulations and no GCA photography judges – just one local photographer whom we asked to judge the photos," recalled Ingrid Conant. As flower show co-chair, Ingrid proposed and organized the photography exhibit. By the 2006 Zone XI Meeting in Kansas City, there were photography classes. "No limit had been placed on the number of entries and there were hundreds," Ingrid said. "I helped hang the photos. They were not judged by judges; delegates chose winners by ballot."

Ingrid, who served as GCA Zone XI Flower Show Chair in 2012, said

that the GCA now requires clubs to include photography in all major and small flower shows, although it's optional in club shows. "Photography has become a big thing nationally," she said. "Members from far and wide enter photographs in flower shows. The classes fill months in advance. It's easy and fun.... Very few entrants in our first show in 2003 printed their

own photos because they didn't have printers. Now, everyone's gone digital."

Most of the early GCA photography judges were floral design judges encouraged to take some training, Ingrid said. She became a full-fledged judge in 2013, having completed the required steps: clerking at several shows, exhibiting photographs and winning awards,

Photo, from left: Photography Committee members Anne Ferrell, Sharon Prokosch, Susan Cross, Ingrid Conant and Maureen Adelman shot photos at Como Park.

and serving as a prospectus judge under the guidance of a lead judge for three years. In fall 2012, Lou Schatz moved up to the Prospectus level in the photography judging program and JoAnne Wahlstrom continued at the Candidate level.

Fledgling Committee

It wasn't until January 2007 that our garden club started a Photography Committee, with Mollie Keys as chair and Pamela Crandall as assistant. Pamela and Ellen Maas Pratt each chaired the committee for two years and JoAnne Wahlstrom is our 2013-2014 chair. The committee educates and encourages members at workshops and membership meetings. Workshops have included "Entering a Flower Show," "Photo Matting" and a "Member Photography Show" at our July 2008 annual meeting. That fall, Judy MacManus taught us to how to enhance and crop our photos and turn them into personalized note cards by using computer software.

In spring 2009, Ingrid and Lou led

a two-part workshop. Members took photos in the Como Park Butterfly Garden and critiqued their photos at a review session. At our "Autumn Joy" Flower Show in September 2009, wildlife photographer Mike Prokosch led a candid discussion of the photo entries. Photographer Don Brenneman entertained and instructed us in February 2010 with a colorful show of his flower and nature photographs.

Some of us may be novices, but we've won a bevy of blue ribbons! Members who have won first-place awards include Ellen, Ingrid, JoAnne, Lou, Pamela and Shari Wilsey. "Shari has just gotten the bug," Ingrid

said. "She won a blue ribbon at the September 2012 Zone XI Meeting in Evanston, Illinois, for a photo that was just perfect: the Marjorie McNeely Conservatory dome against the bluest sky. It was printed in *Focus*, the GCA Photography Committee web magazine."

Win Evokes 'Wow!'

Lou Schatz won the Curator's Photography Award in 2009 at "Florescence," a major flower show sponsored by the Houston Club. "It's given to an exhibit of exceptional merit and, wow, was I excited to receive it! The photo was shadows of birch trees on fresh snow." Lou also

Photos, from left: Judy MacManus helped us turn photos into note cards; Shari Wilsey's Marjorie McNeely Conservatory dome won a blue ribbon.

received the GCA Novice Award at "Show of Summer," a major show in Chicago, and her photo made the cover of *Focus*.

Pamela won Best in Show at the GCA Annual Meeting in Providence,

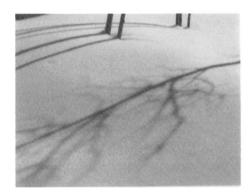

Rhode Island, in 2009. Her entry featured the Saint Paul riverfront viewed from across the Mississippi River. "The Photography Division in GCA Flower Shows is a great avenue for our members to participate in shows across the country," Pamela said. "One can peruse the themes and classes on the GCA website to discover that which sparks one's imagination."

Ellen Maas Pratt won Best in

Show and the GCA Photography Committee Award at our 2009 flower show for a macro showing part of a white dahlia. To encourage members to participate in our club's "The Way We Were" flower show in July 2012, we held a practice flower show in June. Lou and Ingrid critiqued the trial photo entries. The real show schedule

included eight classes with river themes. Susan Brust won a second place and the GCA Novice Award for Photography for a woodland scene near water; and Ingrid, JoAnne, Lou and Susan won blue ribbons.

As photography chair, JoAnne

offers a "Kodak Moment" of practical advice at every club membership meeting. She has a background in graphic design and photography. She started entering GCA photography

Photos, clockwise from left: Award winning photos by Lou Schatz, Pamela Crandall, Susan Brust and Ellen Maas Pratt

shows shortly after she joined our club in 2009, and has won several blues as well as Best in Show in the Spring 2011 *Focus*. "My goal is to encourage whoever has the slightest interest in photography to enter shows and have

for it and I did. While a provisional, I did not tell anyone and submitted a photo in a Lake Geneva Garden Club show and received a second place and Novice Award. I never would have done that but for Ellie's words of encouragement."

Marge Hols

some fun," she said.

"A kind word goes a long way when getting up the courage to enter a photography competition," said Ellen Maas Pratt. "…Members are passionate about their love of photography and very supportive in encouraging new and aspiring photographers. I had never taken a picture of a plant before joining the club. Lou Schatz has been an amazing mentor to me. Ellie Bruner was a huge supporter and told me to go

Photos, clockwise from top: Winning florals by JoAnne Wahlstrom, Ingrid Conant and Bonnie Hollibush.

Mary Stanley: 'Let's Go Tripping!'

Mary Stanley came to the Saint Paul Garden Club in 1986 from the Green Tree Garden Club of Milwaukee. It was said, "Before Mary arrived, this was more a 'social club' and, after Mary, it was a 'Let's go tripping club!'" Mary organized and enthusiastically led us on many trips and adventures.

"It was all about having fun and building camaraderie," Mary said. Trips combined "the social aspect of being together and the opportunity to learn and to continue the education process by broadening our focus." Mary's enthusiasm and knowledge of horticulture made all of these events truly enjoyable and educational.

In 1989, Mary organized a trip back to Milwaukee for the "Art en Fleurs" show. About eight members including Joan Duddingston, Ellen Fridinger and Charlotte Drake signed up. The group attended a preview party and toured private gardens, the Mitchell Park Conservatory, Milwaukee Public Museum Rain Garden and Bradley Sculpture Garden. Mary's schedule offered such wonderful activities that the "Art en Fleurs" judges joined her group.

Ferragamos vs. Tallgrass Prairie

Mary served as horticulture representative for our Zone XI of the Garden Club of America in 1991-93. She was tasked by the GCA horticulture chair to organize a trip to Minnesota for all the GCA horticulture representatives. This included many East Coast members who wondered what could possibly be worth seeing in Minnesota. Mary arranged for the 25 visitors to stay at the Saint Paul Hotel. Faye Duvall hosted a cocktail party for the guests and Mary received them for dinner at her new home in Dellwood.

Mary's events plan kept them moving. The group was taken to Lake Minnetonka to view private

Photo: Mary Stanley (Mrs. Richard W.)

gardens, including an unusual rock garden, and the Minnesota Landscape Arboretum for tours and dinner. The last-day tour was to Lost Prairie, south of Afton, which had been donated by garden club member Marion Fry to the Minnesota Department of Natural Resources. As many of the visitors were planning to catch flights that day and were unaware of the adventure Mary had in mind, they dressed in designer Ultrasuede suits and Ferragamo shoes. Umbrellas completed their outfits as the weather was uncooperatively rainy. To their credit they hiked down a cliff, trudged through tall grasses (warned to watch out for poison ivy) and up a hill. They returned to the East Coast with a good sampling of what Minnesota has to offer.

Elusive Kitten Tails

In 1993 or '94, the GCA had a "Partners for Plants Program" seeking endangered plant species on federal lands. The program inspired Mary to lead a memorable trip to the Minnesota Valley Wildlife Refuge in search of the elusive kitten tails (*Besseya*). Due to flooding, the main route, Highway 169, was impassable by car. It was possible to approach the site only by canoe through what she described as a "raging torrent along the road and under the canopy of trees." Undeterred, Mary made the canoe voyages and portages accompanied by Debbie Bancroft, Lee Driscoll, Marilyn Magid from the Cedar Rapids Garden Club and Judy Milligan-McCarthy from the Des Moines Founders Garden Club. They searched the site for two-and-a-half days using a grid of the area and successfully located the kitten tails.

On another trip, Mary took our members to Lake Geneva, Wisconsin. The group drove south along the Mississippi River and visited the Indian Mounds, an historic house in Mineral Point and Taliesin East. On the return leg, they stopped at the International Crane Foundation. Charlotte Drake, an avid miniature golfer, persuaded the group to detour for a game.

Gentians at Iron Horse Prairie

There was a late-October trip to the naturally conserved Iron Horse Prairie, a tiny, triangular, mesic pocket prairie bounded by railroads tracks in southeastern Minnesota. A planned picnic lunch was threatened by cold, overcast weather. But, just as the group arrived, the sun came out and a sea of blue fringed gentian came forth as a surprise. Mary

Photo: A garden club field trip to a prairie

also led a group to the Savage Fen, a rare wetland plant community, and the Black Dog Prairie in Burnsville.

On a memorable trip in June 2005, 18 club members drove to the Winter Greenhouse in Northern Wisconsin, where they crammed their cars with botanical treasures. The outing included an overnight stay at members' homes along the Brule River. Marla Ordway entertained with a delightful dinner and tour at the Ordway compound.

Mary's Club Philosophy

Mary Stanley's myriad experiences as a super-active member of the Saint Paul Garden Club and the Garden Club of America led her to develop a thoughtful and purposeful philosophy for our garden club. Among her many roles were president of our club in 1990-91, GCA horticulture judge beginning in 1989 and GCA Director in 2005-07.

"The foundation of a garden club is a love of plants, i.e., horticulture," Mary said. "The other activities and committees – photography, conservation, flower arranging – are all based on this love of plants or horticulture.

"As members, we must strive to educate ourselves in all these related areas. Education is the purpose of the club. We give back to the community through this education of our members. The club needs to focus on community involvement – what to do for the community.

"Becoming a member is a choice based on the stage of one's life and the demands of the family. But if joining is based on the love of gardening and a desire to learn more, then one is joining for the right reasons. We need to accommodate the younger members who have children and busy schedules, perhaps by giving assignments they can do at home. We need to offer extras without requiring everyone to participate, so as to avoid burn out. Required participation should be in the areas of large projects the whole club has agreed to tackle. And, of course, someone in the club needs to plan trips."

Deni Svendsen

Photo, from left: Brule River trip included Mary Stanley, Jean Rowland, Ellie Brunner, Julie Titcomb and Marge Hols.

Garden Club Tea Dance
Family Fun and Fundraising

Thirty-plus years since the first Tea Dance, the event's hallmarks continue to delight: Jerry Mayeron's Orchestra plays the Bunny Hop; the dance floor is graced with dancing Christmas trees; and Santa makes an appearance, hearing last-minute wishes from flush-cheeked children sporting balloon animals and sticky fingers.

The primary fundraiser of the Saint Paul Garden Club has taken place the Sunday before Christmas since 1980. The Tea Dance was initially conceived as "a way to socialize my children," said co-founder Susan St. John. She recalled growing up outside New York City, learning company manners and how to dance.

Susan wanted to provide an opportunity for multigenerational families to get together. The primary focus for Susan and the other tea dance founders, Joan Gardner, Twinks Irvine and Judy Diedrich, was a

coalescence of community in Saint Paul.

The first tea dance, attended by 650 people, was held in 1980 at Landmark Center in Saint Paul as a benefit for the center's ongoing restoration. Arthur Murray taught dance lessons; food was generous; table decorations were lush and seasonal; and, above all, the focus was "on first-

rate fun," commented Susan.

Although the Tea Dance didn't begin as a Saint Paul Garden Club event, it soon became one. In 1981, the three founders who were members of the garden club – Joan, Twinks and Susan – decided their organization was the best fit for the event. It was a fortunate coincidence that many members of the club attended the first

Photo: Children danced with the Christmas trees.

party. The structure of that event gave the club something to build on.

This annual party, which over the years raised more than $500,000 for city beautification, community

gardens, conservation and plant development, was deliberately staged to celebrate the good life in Saint Paul.

Through the years, members of the garden club have embraced the event and volunteered countless hours to ensure its success. Table centerpieces designed by the club's talented flower arrangers have been a highlight. These creations, assembled by members, have been as elaborate as lighted topiary teacups filled to the brim with roses; or, as simple, but spectacular, as tall green vases topped with bright amaryllis lilies.

The Tea Dance venue has changed several times, moving from Landmark Center to the Radisson Hotel (now the Crowne Plaza) to the Prom Center in Woodbury. It has been held there since 1998, except for one year at the First Trust Great Hall in Saint Paul.

Susan said it best: "The Tea Dance has been a nice occasion that families can count on every year to celebrate themselves, their children and Saint Paul as a special place to live and enjoy. And that's what is important in creating a lasting event – the soul of the event has to be the first priority and it has to fulfill an authentic purpose or real need. After that the money will inevitably come in."

Children who learned how to

dance at the first Tea Dance now bring their children to this festive holiday tradition. The women who conceived the event remain supporting members of the garden club. They couldn't be more pleased that their vision continues to bring families together and has had a lasting impact on our community.

Roddie Turner

Photos, from left: 2005 Tea Dance Committee: Roddie Turner, Deni Svendsen, Cathy DeCourcy, Julie Whitaker, Lou Schatz, Ingrid Conant, Pam Senkler, Mary Dennis and Judy MacManus; and George Tesar and granddaughter in 1996

Plant Sales
Troves of Memorabilia and Valuables

The Saint Paul Garden Club has used plant sales to underwrite special projects that were not included in its annual budgets. The first Plant and Seedling Sale was held in spring, 1928. "We cleared about $100. It was much more of a success than we dared hope," reported President Linda Ames (Mrs. Charles L.). Funds were used to beautify Saint Paul parks.

The first sale in recent memory was an impromptu affair June 2-3, 2005, when the club realized it needed additional funds for its 2006 flower show. Pam Attia graciously volunteered to use the grounds at her Summit Avenue home for a public garage sale. The planning group decided to launch a "no holds barred" sale of not only plants from members' gardens, but all things garden related.

Members took that literally. Strewn around Pam's garage and lawn when the sale began were everything

from gorgeous plants to an ugly floral chenille robe from Lee Driscoll's college days, which, ironically, brought one of the highest prices! Members brought in a carload from Charlotte Drake, who was ill and wanted to share her garden and flower-arranging treasures. Sale items included gardening books, pottery, floral purses and – a highlight of the sale – an antique Northrup King seed-packet display stand from Bonnie Hollibush that sold for $800. Back to the robe. A young woman dressed in punk style arrived on a mission: Someone had alerted her to the chenille robe and she had to have it. She paid $75 and left with a gleeful smile!

Everything Sold!

Everything sold – even items

Photo, from left front: 2008 Plant Sale Committee: Tracy Stutz and Maureen Adelman; Back row: Mary Gilbertson, Christine Umhoefer, Carol Kolb, Bonnie Hollibush, Marge Hols, Blanche Hawkins

members had shaken their heads over when brought to sell. An impressive profit of $3,145 was made, and club members knew they had hit upon an easy way to raise funds for future special projects.

The June 11, 2008 sale was a grander, more labor-intensive affair. Not only would there be a plant sale, but a beautiful summer outdoor lunch and silent auction at the White Bear Lake home of Blanche Hawkins, where, hopefully, the garden would be in bloom. Members began work on the sale early that year. The logistics were formidable, including providing parking for up to 200 guests.

Questions of where to put the silent auction, and what items to solicit, make or scavenge from members' own troves of memorabilia and valuables were soon solved. The silent auction would take place in the large gallery/foyer and plants would be sold outside in various locations. A highlight of the sale would be rare plants from members' own gardens, mini evergreens from Oregon and

unusual plants that Marge Hols persuaded nursery friends to donate.

As the day grew near, the presale of 125 tickets and the generosity of friends and neighbors ensured a successful sale. Among the wonderful auction items were a cocktail party/garden tour of Colles and John Larkin's renowned garden and a cocktail party/art tour of Dar Reedy's famed art collection. A special item to be auctioned separately was a week at Lucy Dunning's Vail, Colorado, home.

Alas, the day dawned rainy, with sporadic showers, lightening and thunder. Carol Kolb and Blanche wondered how to feed 125 people who were to have been seated outside on a fine June day. Members, their spouses and children hauled tables and chairs inside. We all hoped 25 people would stay away at lunch, as there was room for only 100 at the tables squeezed into every nook and cranny. Most members had brought their plants the day before, and the committee set up tables under a tent and in the garage with labeled, priced plants. Members dressed in layers, with rain gear and umbrellas in full display, and smiles that belied the grim weather conditions.

Photo: Blanche Hawkins, our intrepid hostess

Down Came the Rain

Finally, all was ready. But, just as the first intrepid guest, dressed in a lovely summer frock and heels, strolled up the drive, a clap of thunder resounded, hailing a very long, cold wet day.

Only in Minnesota! One hundred people were seated for lunch. Many more attended the sale, most dressed a bit more practically than the first guest, and cheerfully took off their shoes to come inside for the auction and lunch. Everyone was in good humor and seemed unfazed by the intermittent thunder and rain, which ceased precisely when the sale ended that afternoon. The rest of June was gorgeous.

When all was accounted for, the club raised $9,719 for its 2009 flower show. Blanche found some orphaned plants that had landed in piles around and under the tables. Those plants, which now adorn the Hawkins foyer, symbolize the grace and undaunted spirit with which the committee overcame the difficulties nature presented and staged an unforgettable community event. Many thank-you notes indicated the sale was the most fun attendees had all summer.

In addition to these special projects fund raisers, four May plant sales were held for members only between 2002 and 2005. Ingrid Conant organized the sales and encouraged members to order hanging baskets, flats of bedding plants and specialty annuals, which she obtained from Gertens.

The weather, once again, proved challenging. As brightly colored plants awaited pickup on Ingrid's lawn one mid-May morning, winds picked up, the temperature plunged and snow dusted the plants. "It was so cold," Ingrid recalled, "we were frozen stiff and warmed our hands on our coffee mugs."

Blanche Hawkins

Songbird Needlepoint Rug

A Work of Art

Over the years, the Saint Paul Garden Club has found many enterprising ways to raise funds for its flower shows and philanthropic endeavors. In 1984, club members decided to design and assemble a needlepoint rug to raffle at various venues.

The three-by-five foot rug was composed of eight panels featuring Minnesota songbirds. It was designed by Kitty Parfit with input from Vicky Holman, Larry DeLaHunt, Twinks Irvine and Joan Gardner. Eight members volunteered to stitch one of the panels: Marge Allen, rose grosbeak; Lee Driscoll, robin; Polly Dean, oriole; Julie Titcomb, evening grosbeak; Betty Biorn, purple finch; Lucy Cantwell, brown thrasher; and Twinks Irvine, cardinal. The resulting rug was a work of art!

A total of 2,500 chances were printed and each member was given 30 chances to sell. The price was

$5, or three for $10. Sales began in April, with the raffle to be held at the club's Tea Dance on December 23 at Landmark Center.

Members arranged to sell chances at various locations, including Park Nursery and the Minnesota Landscape Arboretum. They even asked the Lake Minnetonka Garden Club to sell chances at its membership meeting,

but got turned down. Some club members chose to buy all 30 chances rather than ask friends and relatives to contribute. The final push occurred at the Tea Dance, where members' children persuaded attendees to buy, spurred on by Joan Gardner, who made some sales herself.

Then, at last, the much-anticipated drawing was held. The

Photo: Needlepoint rug was designed and stitched by club members in 1984.

rug went to Missy Mears Wilson of Saint Paul, who won with a $10 raffle purchase. She was not a garden club member, and wasn't present at the Tea Dance to claim her beautiful prize.

The raffle was a grand success, with the club raising $4,655.

While writing this history in 2011, members wondered where the rug might be after all these years. The mystery was solved when Andrea McCue remembered seeing it at her friend Missy Wilson's home. She contacted Missy, who said the needlepoint rug has been hanging on her living room-dining room wall ever since she won it 27 years ago. Missy also shared with us the names of the needlepoint artists.

Blanche Hawkins

'You're Going to the Zone Meeting!'

Those are heady words for a Saint Paul Garden Club president who's attended a zone meeting before and enticing to the novice delegate about to embark on her first experience in the upper echelons of the Garden Club of America. They will be traveling to one of the other 18 clubs in GCA Zone XI, where they'll be feted for three jam-packed days. They'll engage in meetings, tours, perhaps a horticulture or flower show, an awards dinner and exciting conversations with new and old friends, and take home a special plant grown by the host club.

Zone XI clubs rotate as hosts every 19 years. Our garden club has hosted wonderful meetings planned hand in hand with the Zone XI officers by some of our most dedicated members. The 1956 zone meeting was referred to as the "Central Western Zone Meeting." Nationally recognized speakers John Rose and Eugene

Hildreth from Keep America Beautiful spoke on litter, the meeting theme. Elizabeth Clark from our club was one of 53 delegates who paid a registration fee of $15, compared with today's fee of $150. Thirty-nine of our dedicated members hosted the entire meeting on a budget of only $2,236.

In June of 1970 Elizabeth Slade and Dorothy Fobes chaired a zone meeting themed "Our Natural Resources." The meeting was headquartered at the Saint Paul Hilton, but delegates were always on the go. Offsite tours included a Flower Exhibit and tour at the Theodore Griggs Home, a guided walk at the Thomas Irvine Dodge Nature Center, visits to two Sunfish Lake gardens, a tour of the Minnesota Landscape

Photo: Colles Larkin, Ingrid Conant and Susan Cross set up a horticulture exhibit at the 2003 Zone XI meeting in Saint Paul.

Arboretum, a Mississippi Riverboat Trip and dinner in private homes on White Bear Lake, an event repeated in every zone meeting our club has hosted.

'Northern Lights' Theme

"Northern Lights" was the theme in September of 1988 as Zone XI delegates gathered at the Saint Paul Hotel. Chairs Tottie Lilly and Larry DeLaHunt packed their days. Features included a Flower Show of only two challenge classes so delegates didn't have to transport flowers and tools. There was a Horticulture Display, a Club Challenge and a Plant Exchange. Dr. James W. Haun, former director of Environmental Affairs at General Mills, moderated a Conservation Meeting on Industry's Environmental Responsibilities. For Saint Paul delegates, the highlight of the Awards Dinner was the presentation of the Zone Conservation Award to Olivia Dodge. Saint Paul delegates were Lucy Fellows, president, and Elsie Hill. Every delegate went home with an

Orchid Lights azalea plant, a recent introduction from the Minnesota Landscape Arboretum.

In 2003 Carol Whitaker Kolb and Betsy Kelly chaired "Rooted and Growing." Mayor Randy Kelly welcomed delegates to the buildings

on Rice Park. There was a Small Flower Show and dinner at the Minnesota Science Museum, meetings in courtrooms at Landmark Center, hospitality at the Saint Paul Hotel and the Awards Dinner at 317 (the former Minnesota Club). An emotional Charlotte Drake received the Zone

Horticulture Award at the dinner. A short bus ride away found the delegates enjoying Swede Hollow, a Hmong lunch, tour and lunch at Gibbs Farm, members' private gardens

Photos, from left: Arnulf and Deni Svendsen with Mayor Randy Kelly; Roddie Turner and her ferris wheel floral design at 2003 GCA Zone Meeting; and Joan Duddingston with her blue-ribbon clematis

and dinners on White Bear Lake. Saint Paul delegates were President Priscilla Brewster and Pam Nuffort, who teamed up in a Flower Show Challenge Class.

Zone meetings are not only a wonderful learning experience, but also an opportunity to meet new friends and future co-workers in GCA. Debbie Bancroft, our club delegate to the 1992 Zone Meeting, summed it nicely when she said, "Sometimes the gracious festivities blind us to the fact that a zone meeting is all about the serious and excellent meetings!"

Marla Ordway

Photos, from left: Marge Hols with her "survivor houseplant" entry at the 2003 show; Anne Zelle and Clover Earl at the 1985 GCA Zone XI Meeting in Forest Lake, Illinois; and Joan Duddingston's garden, on tour of members' gardens

Scholarships
Encouraging Future Gardeners

The Garden Club of America (GCA) awarded its first scholarship in 1928. As of 2010, it awards 24 scholarships totaling $200,000 every year. Every club has a scholarship chair who promotes the GCA scholarships to local colleges and universities. The Saint Paul Garden Club has contributed annually to the GCA scholarship fund.

We have records of two scholarships established by our own club over the years. The first, in 1953, was a Yale Conservation scholarship at Yale University's Graduate School of Conservation in New Haven, Connecticut. The two-year grant, totaling $1,500, was created and financed by our club and administered by the Minnesota Conservation Commissioner.

In 2006, our garden club established a scholarship honoring Charlotte Drake, who passed away the previous year. During her 25 years as a member of our club, Charlotte served in many capacities, including president in 1996-98 (see Charlotte Drake profile).

The club also donated $2,000 in 2009 to the GCA scholarship fund to honor Mary Stanley, a dynamic club member who moved to Milwaukee. Funds were used for a summer internship for a student studying horticulture in our GCA Zone XI. Mary served in many capacities, including club president in 1990-91 (see Mary Stanley profile).

Ingrid Conant

The Garden Club's Book Club

As we entered the new century, a Book Club was started by the Horticulture Committee of the Saint Paul Garden Club. Members who participated recall stimulating discussions and good times.

"I believe we felt a bit insignificant in that era when the greatest emphasis in the club was on flower arranging," recalled Joan Duddingston, who hosted one of the meetings. "There were many significant arrangers/mentors leading us 'learners.' But, we wanted to remember that growing flowers and understanding their cultures was part of the gardening game, so we decided to attack it intellectually by reading. Well, that was the theory, anyway."

Our first meeting was at the Dellwood home of Mary Stanley, who suggested the club. "We discussed the book, planned our next meeting and selection, and then had lunch," Susan Cross said. "We each brought

a sandwich and Mary provided soup and fruit, setting the trend for future meetings. There wasn't a specific group; any member could attend.

"The first book was *Night Gardening* by E.L. Swann, pen name of Katherine Lasky," Susan said. "It was much appreciated by all the gardeners who indulged. Roddie Turner suggested the book, which was about

a retired lady who lives in a home in Boston with a lovely back garden, and then meets and falls in love with the man whose is landscaping the garden next door to hers."

Ethel Griggs recalled a good discussion of *The Orchid Thief, a True Story of Beauty and Obsession*, by Susan Orlean, and another book on orchids "while sitting amidst the

Photo, from left: Master Gardener Gretchen Lindgren entertained Susan Cross, Paula Soholt, Ethel Griggs, Ingrid Conant and Joan Duddingston at her home and garden near Saint Cloud.

wonderful orchids blooming in Ruth Huss's greenhouse room. We brought our own sandwiches and all was very casual."

Another book Susan remembered reading was *A Clearing in the Distance: Frederick Law Olmsted and America in the 19th Century* by Witold Rybczynski. "It's a very interesting biography of the Olmsted brothers and the gardens and parks they designed and landscaped," she said.

A Prodigal Summer by Barbara Kingsolver was discussed over lunch at Patti Saunder's cabin on Love Lake after a field trip to a nearby nature preserve. That book sparked some controversy.

When members gathered in the spring of 2003 at Susan's home on Bald Eagle Lake, they discussed *The Wild Gardener, the Life and Selected Writings of Eloise Butler*. In May, the group toured the Eloise Butler Wildflower Garden in Minneapolis. Marge Hols, new to the group,

remembered Mary Stanley identifying trout lilies, marsh marigolds, skunk cabbage and other native plants along the pathways.

"I really enjoyed the combination of reading and field trip to the Eloise Butler garden," Ethel said. "The book club was a great way to meet with just a few members and discuss plants and gardens in a different way. I'm not sure why we stopped meeting."

Inspired by Mary Stanley's tripping, in June 2004, the Horticulture Committee teamed with the Book Club to plan a trip to Saint Cloud's Munsinger and Clemens Gardens. Among the trekkers were Ingrid Conant, Susan Cross, Joan Duddingston, Ethel Griggs, Marge Hols and Paula Soholt. The outing included lunch and a tour of Master Gardener Gretchen Lindgren's delightful country garden near Saint Cloud.

After a few years, the time the group spent actually discussing books waned, Joan recalled. "The pull of

the hostess' garden was too much, and the book reviews began to slide into garden reviews and perhaps an exciting field trip or two. But, even if we didn't stick to the original path, we had a wonderful time, as dirt gardeners, exchanging cultivating tips, new discoveries of seeds, et al., and just enjoying the company of like-minded members."

Marge Hols

Hybrid Daylily Project
'One-Thousand Seeds for One Stunner'

When Saint Paul Garden Club members carpooled to Karol Emmerich's daylily breeding farm in Jordan in 2006, little did we know we were about to embark on growing hybridized daylilies from seed.

Karol's operation, called Springwood Gardens, is focused on developing fancy daylilies – the kind usually found only in warm climates – that will survive in northern gardens. The daylilies she has introduced have large blossoms, beautiful color combinations and, usually, ruffled margins.

"I harvest 25,000 hybrid seeds each year from my test gardens and plant about 5,000 seeds," Karol told us. That prompted Marge Hols, horticulture co-chair, to ask if Karol would be willing to give garden club members some of her extra seeds. She would!

Thus began the club's hybrid daylily project. More than 20 members signed up and planted a packet of seeds

in January through March 2007. All the seeds had the same "Dad" (pollen parent), but a different "Mom" (pod parent).

The first plant bloomed in July in horticulture chair Bonnie Hollibush's Marine on Saint Croix garden. Bonnie's best daylily bloomed the next summer—a striking plant with a pink and chartreuse throat

and burgundy petals edged in creamy ruffles. Many other members' seedlings bloomed, too, and have survived year after year. Some are a fabulous blend of colors with ruffles, but others are quite ordinary, as Karol had told us to expect.

"I have to plant 1,000 hybrid seeds to get one absolute stunner," said Karol.

Marge Hols

Photo: Springwood Gardens hybrid daylily

Celebrating Our 75th and 80th Anniversaries

Special occasions deserve specially planned events and the Saint Paul Garden Club made festive arrangements for both its 75th and 80th Anniversaries. We celebrated our 75th at the club's annual meeting in July 2002 at the White Bear Yacht Club. Members dressed in retro or vintage styles featuring hats and gloves harkening back to the days of our founders in 1927. They presented a play called "Charlotte's Dream," which was discovered in the club archives. It depicted a fictionalized account of members awaiting the decision for the club to be accepted into the Garden Club of America (GCA) in 1933.

Charlotte Ordway wrote in her *Short History*, "It seemed a long time before we heard from the National. Margaret Wright (Mrs. Cushing) wrote a charming play on our troubles and worries over the possibility that we'd been turned down. The day we

were to give the play at a meeting, word came by telegraph from the National President welcoming us to membership! I think, in our excitement, we had more than tea and cookies in celebration."

At our 75th Anniversary, members enthusiastically took the roles in the play wearing period costumes. Mary Stanley evoked high drama in her

role as Charlotte, then president of the garden club, traveling to GCA headquarters in New York by train and fretting over the possibility of our club being rejected. The member-audience was delighted and applauded our thespians' performance.

The 80th Anniversary celebration in 2007 was again set for our annual meeting and held at the White Bear

144

Photo: Garden club's 75th Anniversary brought together 14 club presidents (see page 145 for names).

Yacht Club, a lovely venue offering a view of White Bear Lake. It was a perfect Minnesota day in July. Clover

Earl and Vicky Holmen arranged an in-house flower show. Ellie Bruner planned and moderated a style show featuring garden club members dressed in outfits from each of the club's

eight decades. It was a glamorous and effective way to evoke memories of the past. Ellie also compiled a booklet outlining the history of the club including memorable photos, which was given to members. The table centerpieces were birthday cakes decorated with fresh flowers, which served as luncheon desserts. There

may even have been champagne and, certainly, toasts to "continued years of gardening, friendship and community."

These celebrations and remembrances have proved to be an important way to nurture the spirit of our club as well as being a lot of fun.

Deni Svendsen

Club presidents, from page 144:
From left front: Priscilla Brewster, Carol Kolb, Marla Ordway, Lee Driscoll; back, Faye Duvall, Julie Titcomb, Clover Earl, Lucy Dunning, Carolyn DeCoster, Charlotte Drake, Lucy Fellows, Marge Ordway, Mary Stanley and Tottie Lilly
Member Models:
Pam Attia, Jean Rowland, Ruth Huss, Cathy DeCourcy, Faye Duvall, Pam Nuffort, Blanche Hawkins, Marge Hols and Joan Duddingston

Photos, from left: Member–Models at 80th Anniversary (see right for names); Deni Svendsen, Lou Schatz, Ellie Bruner costumed for 75th Anniversary; and club presidents Priscilla Brewster and Marla Ordway at 75th.

Saint Paul Garden Club Presidents

1927-28	Linda Ames (Mrs. Charles Lesley)		1973-75	Margaret Ordway (Mrs. John G., Jr.)
1928-29	Miss Helen Bunn		1975-77	Louise Benz (Mrs. George W.)
1929-30	Frances Daniels (Mrs. Thomas L.)		1977-79	Elisabeth Ljungkull (Mrs. Rolf G.)
1930-32	Geraldine Thompson (Mrs. Horace)		1979-81	Julie Titcomb (Mrs. Edward R.)
1932-34	Charlotte Ordway (Mrs. John G., Sr.)		1981-83	Betty Biorn (Mrs. Norman E.)
1934-35	Kathleen Gates (Mrs. Stanley)		1982-83	Polly Jackson (Mrs. John N.)
1935-37	Margaret Wright (Mrs. Cushing F.)		1983-84	Larry DeLaHunt (Mrs. Stanley)
1937-38	Edith Brooks (Mrs. Springer)		1984-84	Tottie Lilly (Mrs. James T.)
1938-40	Geraldine Thompson (Mrs. Horace)		1985-86	Clover Earl (Mrs. George R.)
1940-42	Anne White (Mrs. Edwin)		1986-87	Elizabeth Driscoll (Mrs. W. John)
1942-44	Helen Baird (Mrs. Julian)		1987-88	Ann Zelle (Mrs. Louis N.)
1944-46	Arlene Griggs (Mrs. Milton Wright)		1988-89	Mrs. Lucy Fellows
1946-47	Charlotte Ordway (Mrs. John G., Sr.)		1989-90	Carolyn DeCoster (Mrs. Donald, Jr.)
1947-49	Clotilde Irvine (Mrs. Horace Hills)		1990-91	Mary Stanley (Mrs. Richard W.)
1949-51	Carolyn Lindeke (Mrs. Albert W.)		1991-93	Faye Duvall (Mrs. Arndt J., III)
1951-53	Mary Ward (Mrs. William E.)		1993-95	Lucy Dunning (Mrs. Peter B.)
1953-55	Elizabeth Slade (Mrs. G. Norman)		1995-96	Betty Tiffany (Mrs. Francis B.)
1955-57	Annetta Morgan (Mrs. John E.P.)		1996-98	Charlotte Drake (Mrs. Carl B., Jr.)
1957-59	Roberta Gardner (Mrs. Truman P.)		1998-00	Carol Whitaker (Mrs. Ron Kolb)
1959-61	Katherine Clarkson (Mrs. Worrell)		2000-02	Marla Ordway (Mrs. John G., III)
1961-63	Peggy Jackson (Mrs. Archibald B.)		2002-04	Priscilla Brewster
1963-65	Marjorie McNeely (Mrs. Donald G.)		2004-06	Ingrid Conant (Mrs. Roger R.)
1965-67	Eunice Butler (Mrs. Francis D.)		2006-08	Ellen Bruner (Mrs. Philip L.)
1967-69	Libby Clark (Mrs. Robert D.)		2008-10	Ellen Fridinger (Mrs. Tomas L.)
1969-71	Ruth Shepard (Mrs. S. MacMillan, Jr.)		2010-12	Judy MacManus (Mrs. Gary)
1971-72	Clotilde Moles (Mrs.Edwin J., Jr.)		2012-	Catherine Nicholson (Mrs. Ford J.)
1972-73	Alice Weed (Mrs. George)			

Awards

'How Can We Thank You for All You Have Done?'

We can publicly express our gratitude and honor you. We can present you with an award to acknowledge your accomplishments as a volunteer. We can't even begin to estimate the financial value of your efforts. But we can recognize your many hours of work, which have created so much of value for our club and our community. We applaud all of you for following our founders' lead in embracing volunteerism as an avocation that benefits the community at large.

Deni Svendsen

Awards Given to the Saint Paul Garden Club and Members In Recognition of Contributions within the Club, to GCA and to the Twin Cities

1944   Garden Club is awarded a Certificate "in Grateful Recognition of Distinguished War Service in Cooperation with USO."

1961   SPGC awarded a Bronze Medal by the Minnesota State Historical Society for promotion and support of the Minnesota Landscape Arboretum.

1977   SPGC was awarded $6,500 from Garden Club of America Founders Fund for Swede Hollow.

1985   SPGC was awarded Honorable Mention by GCA for the landscape design of Swede Hollow.

1987   SPGC received an Appreciation Award from the Head Start Child Development Center for fine work, flower garden, trees, etc.

1987   SPGC and Lake Minnetonka received the Joint Flower Show award from GCA.

1990   Certificate of appreciation was awarded the SPGC from the State of Minnesota and Gov. Rudy Perpich "for the fine efforts and beautiful contributions of SPGC volunteers at the Governor's mansion."

1990   SPGC received the GCA Flower Show Award "for distinction in the aesthetic arrangement and perfection of display of quality of plant material."

1991   SPGC received an award "in grateful recognition" for the Fringed Orchid from the Center for Plant Conservation.

1994   SPGC was awarded one brick used in the landscape of the Center for Northern Gardening, Falcon Heights by the Minnesota State Horticultural Society.

1995   SPGC and Saint Paul Division of Parks and Recreation received the Minnesota Recreation and Park Association Award for excellence in contributing to community livability, Swede Hollow, Olivia Dodge, organizer.

1995   SPGC received the "President's award for outstanding contribution to Minnesota Green" from the Minnesota State Horticultural Society.

1995   SPGC received a Certificate of Commendation from Gov. Arne Carlson for helping rejuvenate the community through the Minn. Green Program.

2000   SPGC was acknowledged for a generous donation to GCA's Project 2000 Outdoor Classroom and Butterfly Garden in Washington, D.C.

2001   Gibbs Farm was a finalist for GCA Founders Fund.

2002   GCA awarded recognition and congratulations to the SPGC for its 75th Anniversary.

2003   SPGC was awarded the first of 3 Star Grant awards for Blooming Saint Paul.

2005   SPGC received the Garden Club of the Year award by Minnesota State Horticultural Society.

2005   SPGC and Saint Paul Parks & Recreation received the Environmental Improvement Merit Award for Excellence in Landscaping for Kellogg Boulevard Beautification from the Minnesota Nursery and Landscape Association.

2006   SPGC received a thank you for the Minn. Women's Building Garden from Minn. Women's Consortium and the League of Women Voters.

2007   The garden of SPGC member Colles Larkin and her husband John Larkin was accepted into the Smithsonian Archives of American Gardens.

2007   SPGC received an award from the Great River Greening, "Non-Profit Environmental Steward of the Year."

2011   Rice Park Saint Paul designated one of the "Great Places in America, Public Spaces" by the American Planning Association.

Saint Paul Garden Club Members Honored for Their Contributions

1971   Olivia Dodge received the GCA National Award for Thomas Irvine Dodge Nature Center.

2003   Betsy Kelly received the City of Saint Paul Civic Improvement Award for Blooming Saint Paul.

2006   Marge Hols received the Governor's Certificate of Recognition from Gov. Tim Pawlenty for "exceptional contributions in helping rejuvenate your community environment and livability."

2011   Maureen Adelman received the Minnesota State Horticultural Society Life Award for her creative and focused leadership as a board member and president of the society, and as a director and president of the Garden Club of Ramsey County.

2012   Faye Duvall received Minnesota State Horticultural Society Life Award for exhibiting leadership in MSHS and the Saint Paul Garden Club for 30 years.

GCA AWARDS

Club Appreciation Award

1999	Betsy Kelly (Mrs. A. David)
2001	Leslie Carnes (Mrs. Norris) and Jean Rowland (Mrs. John)
2004	Carol Kolb (Mrs. Ron)
2005	Sally Brown (Mrs. Chris)
2006	Julie Whitaker (Mrs. Charles)
2007	Ingrid Conant (Mrs. Roger)
2008	Tracy Stutz (Mrs. Todd)
2009	Judy MacManus (Mrs. Gary)
2010	Marge Hols (Mrs. David)
2011	Nancy Scherer (Ken Collier)
2012	Maureen Adelman (Mrs. Ira)
2013	Alex Bjorklund and Nancy Field (Mrs. Litton E.S.)

Club Conservation Award

1999	Catherine Nicholson (Mrs. Ford)
2001	Betty Tiffany (Mrs. Francis B.)
2005	Colles Larkin (Mrs. John)
2008	Pegi Harkness (Mrs. Thomas)
2010	Andrea McCue (Mrs. Steven)
2012	Blanche Hawkins (Mrs. Thane)

Club Historic Preservation Award

1981	Carolyn DeCoster received a Certificate of Merit for Historic Preservation.

1998 Priscilla Farnham, Executive Director, Community Design Center of Minnesota received SPGC Non-Member Historic Preservation Award.

2003	Charlotte Drake (Mrs. Carl B., Jr.)
2013	Deni Svendsen (Mrs. Arnulf L.)

GCA Medal of Honor to Non-Members

1998	Dr. Harold Pellett, Professor, University of Minnesota; Executive Director, Landscape Plant Development Center
2010	Peter Olin, Executive Director, University of Minnesota Landscape Arboretum

GCA Honorary Member

2010	Dr. Harold Pellet, Professor, University of Minnesota

Club Floral Design Award

2000	Marge Ordway (Mrs. John G., Jr.)
2001	Lucy Fellows
2002	Betty Cammack (Mrs. Malcolm)
2003	Barbara Braman Bentson (Mrs. Lawrence)
2007	Clover Earl (Mrs. George R.)
2008	Sharon Prokosch (Mrs. Richard)
2010	Nancy Hilger (Mrs. Nicholas)
2011	Pam Nuffort (Mrs. Robert)
2012	Christine Umhoefer (Mrs. David)

Club Horticulture Award

1993	Elisabeth Ljungkull (Mrs. Rolf G.)
1998	Ann McMillan (Mrs. Douglas)
2000	Lucy Dunning (Mrs. Peter)
2001	Ingrid Conant (Mrs. Roger)
2006	Marge Hols (Mrs. David)
2007	Joan Duddingston
2008	Bonnie Hollibush (Mrs. Daniel)
2009	Mary Gilbertson (Mrs. Peter)
2011	Colleen FitzPatrick (Mrs. Kevin Murphy)
2013	Nancy Scherer (Ken Collier)

Medal of Merit

1990	Louise Benz (Mrs. George W.)
1994	Lee Driscoll (Mrs. W. John)
1995	Mary Stanley (Mrs. Richard)
1999	Julie Titcomb (Mrs. Edward)
2001	Charlotte Drake (Mrs. Carl B., Jr.)
2007	Faye Duvall (Mrs. Arndt J., III)
2013	Carol Kolb (Mrs. Ron)

Marion Thompson Fuller Brown Conservation Award

1995	Ellen Fridinger (Mrs. Tomas) and Colles Larkin (Mrs. John E.)

The Garden Club of America Public Relations Commendation Award

Awarded to the Saint Paul Garden Club for the "Autumn Joy" flower show. Public Relations Presentation prepared by Sarah Meek and Judy MacManus.

ZONE AWARDS
Zone Conservation Award

1988	Olivia Dodge (Mrs. Arthur M.)

Zone Creative Leadership Award

2007	Mary Stanley (Mrs. Richard)

Zone Horticulture Award

1993	Marion Fry (Mrs. Robert L.)
1996	Mary Stanley (Mrs. Richard)
2003	Charlotte Drake (Mrs. Carl B., Jr.)

Zone Flower Arrangement Award

2001	Clover Earl (Mrs. George)

Zone Director's Award

2013	Anne Ferrell (Mrs. Charles)

Zone Horticultural Certificate of Acknowledgement to Non-Member

1998	Dr. Harold Pellett, Professor, University of Minnesota

Zone Conservation Certificate of
Acknowledgement to Non-Member

2003   Great River Greening

SAINT PAUL GARDEN CLUB AWARDS

City of Saint Paul Civic Improvement Award

2003   Betsy Kelly (Mrs. A. David)

St. Paul Garden Club Special Appreciation Award

2010   Lori Schindler
2010   Karine Pouliquen
2010   Ron Kolb
2010   Sandra Boardman
2010   Marnie Donnelly
2010   Elisabeth Ljungkull (Mrs. Rolf G.)
2010   Julie Titcomb (Mrs. Edward R.)
2012   Shari Wilsey (Mrs. Roger D.)

Roberta Galloway Gardner Award

1982   Lee Driscoll (Mrs. W. John)
1983   Polly Dean (Mrs. George)
1984   Elisabeth Ljungkull (Mrs. Rolf G.)
1985   Julie Titcomb (Mrs. Edward R.)
1994   Lucy Fellows
1995   Charlotte Drake (Mrs. Carl B., Jr.)
1996   Tottie Lilly (Mrs. James T.)
1997   Mary Stanley (Mrs. Richard)

1998   Marla Ordway (Mrs. John G. III)
1999   Faye Duvall (Mrs. Arndt J. III)
2000   Ellie Bruner (Mrs. Philip)
2001   Priscilla Brewster
2002   Deb Irvine
2003   Carol Kolb (Mrs. Ron)
2004   Deni Svendsen (Mrs. Arnulf L.)
2005   Ethel Griggs (Mrs. Chauncey)
2006   Catherine Nicholson (Mrs. Ford)
2007   Pamela Nuffort (Mrs. Robert)
2008   Judy MacManus (Mrs. Gary)
2009   Maureen Adelman (Mrs. Ira)
2010   Anne Ferrell (Mrs. Charles)
2011   Jean Haut (Mrs. Wayne)
2012   Bonnie Hollibush (Mrs. Daniel)
2013   Judy MacManus (Mrs. Gary)

Saint Paul Garden Club Flower Show Awards

Our members have won literally thousands of ribbons, from Best of Show to a third place award for exhibits in horticulture, floral design and photography at the garden club's many flower shows over the years. In addition, the club has received many Judges' Commendations from the Garden Club of America for our flower show exhibits.

Sharing a National Vision
Members Who Served in Garden Club of America Positions

Priscilla Brewster
  Horticulture Judge, 2012-
  Horticulture Committee, Chair, 2005-07

Eunice Butler (Mrs. Francis D.)
  National Flower Show Judge, 1965
  Accredited Flower Show Judge, 1969

Ingrid Conant (Mrs. Roger R.)
  Scholarship Commitee, Zone Rep, 2007-09
  Awards Committee, Zone Rep, 2009-11
  Flower Show Committee, Zone Rep, 2011-13
  Photography Judge, 2013-

Charlotte Drake (Mrs. Carl B., Jr.)
  Horticulture Judge
  Horticulture Committee, Zone Rep, 2000-01
  Judging Committee, Zone Rep, 2004-05

Clover Earl (Mrs. George R.)
  Flower Arranging Judge
  GCA Flower Arranging Magazine,
  Secretary, 1972-75

Anne Ferrell (Mrs. Charles S.)
  Finance Committee, Member, 2008-11
  Finance Committee, Chair, 2011-14
  GCA Treasurer, Executive Committee,
  2011-14

Carol Kolb (Mrs. Ron)
  Horticulture Judge, 2002-
  Judging Committee, AreaVice-Chair,
  2010-12

Colles Larkin (Mrs. John E.)
  Conservation/NAL Committees, Zone Rep,
  2007-09
  Conservation Committee, Vice-Chair,
  Agriculture, 2009-11

Annetta D. Morgan (Mrs. John E. P.)
  Director, 1958-61

Charlotte Ordway (Mrs. John G., Sr.)
  Director, 1940-43
  Zone XI, Vice-Chair, 1945
  Zone XI, Chair, 1948-50

Marge Ordway (Mrs. John G., Jr.)
  Flower Arranging Judge, 1989
  Admissions Committee, Zone Rep

Marla Ordway (Mrs. John G., III)
  Zone XI, Vice-Chair, 2004-05

Lou Schatz, (Mrs. James E.)
  Photography Judging Candidate, 2010

Ruth Shepard (Mrs. S. MacMillan, Jr.)
  Director, 1972-75

Mary Stanley (Mrs. Richard W.)
  Horticulture Judge, 1989-
  Horticulture Committee, Zone Rep, 1991-93
  Horticulture Committee, Co-Chair,
  Plant Exchange, 1993-95
  Horticulture Committee Liaison to
  Partners for Plants, 1995-97

Medals & Awards Committee,
  Zone Rep, 1997-99
Nominating Committee, Zone Rep,
  1999-2000
Judging Committee, Zone Rep, 2001-03
Admissions Committee, Zone Rep, 2003-05
Director, 2005-07
Judging Committee, Zone Rep, 2007-09

JoAnne Wahlstrom (Mrs. John)
  Photography Judging Candidate, 2011

'...Together We Can Do So Much'
Members of the Saint Paul Garden Club, 1927-2013

The history of the Saint Paul Garden Club would not be complete without acknowledging all of its members. It is these women, who over many years, contributed to the projects and accomplishments described in this book. Through their collaborations and hands-on work, they also forged lifelong friendships. While this history profiles only a few of our leaders, many more made equal or greater contributions to the garden club. We're grateful to all our members, whose efforts have nurtured the growth of our club. They have proved the truth of member Olivia Irvine Dodge's words, "Alone we can do little; together we can do so much."

Christine Umhoefer and Deni Svendsen

Abbott, Daisy Thomson (John S.) 1934
Adelman, Maureen Kelly (Ira) 2006
Alexander, Mary W. (John E.) 1955
Allen, Marjorie (Andrews) 1980
*Ames, Linda Baker (Charles Lesley) 1931
Anderson, Katherine (Robert) 2013
Baird, Helen (Julian B.) 1935
Bancroft, Debbie Butler (Richard H., Jr.) 1982
Barnes, Bertha (Harry G.) 1958
Beek, Grace (Harvey O.) 1969

Bend, Glenn (Harold P.)1928
Benz, Karen (George B.) 1984
Benz, Louise Bremer (George W.) 1958
Bigelow, Virginia Dousman (F.R.) 1937
Biorn, Betty (Norman E.) 1968
Blodgett, Bonnie (Cameron H.) 1995/2010
Boardman, Sandra 1962
Booth, Kate (John) 2009
Bourne, Kathy (Michael) 2013
Braman, Barbara (Edwin C.) 1990
　Bentson, Barbara (Lawrence)
Bratnober, Patricia R. 1990
　Saunders, Patricia R. (Barney)
Brewster, Eunice (Frederick) 1945
　Butler, Eunice (Francis D.)
Brewster, Priscilla 1991
Brooks, Markell Conley (Edward) 1931
Brooks, Edith W. (Springer) (Frederick) 1938
Brown, Sally Cardozo (Chris) 1991
Bruner, Ellen (Philip) 1996
Brust, Susan (Thomas) 2005
Budd, Frannie (John M.) 1952
Bunn, Helen 1928
Burch, Conradine Sanborn (Dr. Frank E.) 1937
Butler, Frannie (Laurence) 1955
　Williams, Frannie (Walter)
Butler, Janine D. (Pierce III) 1969
Cammack, Edna (Howard E.) 1954
Cammack, Elizabeth Bancroft (Malcolm E.) 1977
Cantwell, Lucy Jackson (Samuel H.) 1977
Cardozo, Caroline (Grant Fleming) 2000
Cardozo, Diane Kueffner (Hart N., Jr.) 1973
　Whitten, Diane (Richard W.)
　Weinfurtner, Diane (Edward)
　Roth, Diane (Paul)
Carnes, Lesley (Norris W.) 1989
Christian, Betty B. (Henry B.) 1937
Clark, Elizabeth/Libby (Robert D.) 1952

Clarkson, Katherine (Worrell) 1962
Cleary, Brenda (Bill Jepson) 2013
Closmore, Elizabeth Cammack (Greg) 2013
Cole, Mary (Wallace H.) 1944
Colletti, Catherine (Dick) 2009
Comfort, Helen (James O.) 1984
Conant, Ingrid (Roger) 1997
Cowie, Betty (Henry) 1981
Crandall, Angel (Jake) 2003
Crandall, Pamela (Michael) 2006
Cross, Susan Griggs 1989
Crump, Leigh (Harold) 1995
Cudworth, Gertrude H. (Roger L.) 1940
Daniels, Amelia Leonard (John W.) 1931
Daniels, Frances Mertens (Thomas L.) 1931
Davidson, Mimi (Robert J.) 1979
Davis, Catherine (Edwin W.) 1947
Davis, Kelly (Edward P.) 1968
Dean, Polly (George W.) 1955
DeCoster, Carolyn (Donald, Jr.) 1984
DeCoster, Georgia R. (Donald, Jr.) 1975
　Lindeke, Georgia R.
DeCourcy, Cathy (Donald) 1995
DeLaHunt, Larry (Stanley G.) 1973
Dennis, Mary (Clarence) 1997
Derauf, Alma (Donald E.) 1971
Devereaux, Diana 1989
Diekmann, Becky (Paul) 2009
Dodge, Olivia Irvine (Arthur M.) 1967
Donnelly, Marnie (Stan D., Jr.) 1970
Dosdall, Pat H. (Thomas) 1974
Dotty, Pamela Jean
　Attia, Pamela Dotty 1991
Drake, Charlotte (Carl B., Jr.) 1980
Drake, Franny (Carl B., Jr.) 1960
Drake, Emma B. (H.T.) 1931
Driscoll, Elizabeth/Lee Slade (W. John) 1973
Duddingston, Joan R. 1987

Dunning, Lucy (Peter B.) 1985
Duvall, Faye (Arndt J. III) 1983
Earl, Clotilde/Clover Fobes (George R.) 1970
Elert, Sally (Gerald) 1987
Elsholtz, Marilee (Robert) 2008
Emerson, Diane 1991
Felder, Jeanne (Davitt A.) 1991
Fellows, Lucy 1977
Ferrell, Anne (Charles) 2004
Ffolliott, Gertrude Hill Boeckmann (Peter) 1963
Field, Nancy (Litton E.S.) 1971
Fifield, Marty (F. Thomas) 1965
Fisher, Shirley (Lyle H.) 1965
FitzPatrick, Colleen (Kevin Murphy) 2007
Flandrau, Grace H. (Blair) 1946
Fobes, Dorothy/Simpy (William H., Jr.) 1955
Fobes, Caroline W. (W.H.) 1940
Foley, Jean (Edward) 1931
Foley, Elizabeth Dearth (Frederick E.B.) 1928
Foote, Martha Ann/Hank (Jack C.) 1967
Ford, Josephine Henry (Silas M.) 1941
Foster, Betty (Wood R.) 1967
Fridinger, Ellen (Tomas L.) 1985
Fry, Marion (Robert L.) 1960
Gardner, Joan (James P.) 1977
Gardner, Roberta (Truman P.) 1952
Gates, Kathleen Thompson (Stanley) 1931
Gatto, Emily (Daniel) 2005
Gehan, Lucy (Mark) 2005
Gilbertson, Mary (Peter) 2005
Gillin, Mary (Peter) 2005
Gordon, Adelaide (C. Richards) 1963
Graves, Gertrude (William G.) 1937
Green, Anne (Ronald) 1980
Grieve, Flo (Pierson M.) 1989
Griggs, Mary (C.E. Bayliss) 1971
Griggs, Ethel (Chauncey) 2000
Griggs, Arline Bayliss (Milton Wright) 1931
Griggs, Mary Livingston (Theodore W.) 1935
Guyer, Mary (Reynolds W.) 1984
Halden, Betsy (Peter C.) 2007
Hallowell, Barbara Griggs 1995

Hammes, Mary (Ernest M., Jr.) 1965
Hammond, Eleanor (J. Felton) 1928
Hannaford, Caroline Schurmeier (Jule M., Jr.) 1928/46
Hannaford, Barbara (Jule M.III) 1967
  Bakewell, Barbara (Edward L., Jr.)
Hardenberg, Ianthe (George) 1928
Harkness, Pegi (Tom) 2004
Harmon, Carolyn (Albert H.) 1932
Harmon, Kay (Reuel) 1942
Hanstein, Cornelia (Jack E.) 1941
Harris, Anne (Lawrence R.) 1982
Harris, Clare (B. Burnham) 1952
Harris, Jean (Lincoln) 1963
Harrison, Alice (John G.) 1965
Haut, Jean (Wayne A.) 2007
Hawkins, Blanche (Thane D.) 2001
Hayes, Sue (Lawrence) 1989
Hier, Peggy (Mark B.) 1999
Hilger, Nancy Carney (Nicholas) 2003
Hill, Elsie (Louis W., Jr.) 1952
Hill, Mary Ann (Louis F.) 1985
Hoffman, Brenda (John) 2012
Hollibush, Bonnie (Daniel) 2004
Holmen, Victoria Galloway (Douglas J.) 1974
Hols, Marge (David R.) 2002
Hooley, Colleen (John) 2007
Hubbard, Karen (Stanley G.) 1983
Hunter, Helen H. (Croil) 1954
Huss, Ruth (Alvin John, Jr.) 1984
Irvine, Debra (Horace H. III) 1995
Irvine, Clotilde McCullough (Horace Hills) 1931
Irvine, Sally Ordway (Thomas E.) 1941
Irvine, Sandi (Thomas E., Jr.) 1982
Irvine, Twinks (John O.) 1975
Jackson, Peggy (Archibald B.) 1952
Jackson, Polly (John N.) 1971
Jackson, Beth (Peter) 1995/2010
Jacobson, Barbara (Allen F.) 1989
Juechter, Rebecca (W. Matthew) 1987
Kalman, Alexandra (C. Oscar) 1928

Kellogg, Clara Cook (Frank B.) 1931
Kelly, Betsy (A. David) 1996
Keys, Mollie 1999
King, Peggy (Lawrence H.) 1998
Klein, Grace Trask (Horace) 1931
Kling, Sally (William) 1987
Kriesel, Valerie (Marshall) 1991
Kueffner, Helen Schutte (William) 1931
Langford, Anne (William) 1991
Larkin, Colles Baxter (Dr. John E.) 1983
Lightner, Carrie Drake (William Hurley) 1931
Lilly, Tottie (James T.) 1976
Lilly, Rachel Cunningham (Richard C.) 1931
Lindeke, Carolyn (Albert W.) 1941
Lindeke, Helen (Albert W., Jr.) 1963
Ljungkull, Elisabeth/Peter (Rolf G.) 1966
Lueck, Susan (Bruce) 1987
Lund, Carolynn (Trip) 1999
Maas Pratt, Ellen (Leonard Pratt) 2006
MacLaren, Katherine Dean (Archibald) 1931
MacManus, Judy (Gary) 2001
Maher, Janet (Durand) 1974
Mairs, Florence (George) 1967
Martin, Nancy (Robert R.) 1989
McCarthy, Susan Brewster (Edwin J.) 1993
McCarthy, Alexandra Ordway (J. Daniel) 1971
  Bjorklund, Alexandra O. (Warren)
McComb, Donna (Carter) 1994
McCormick, Judith (Stanley) 2003
McCue, Andrea (Steven) 2006
McDonald, Patricia (Malcolm) 2006
McLaughlin, Sis (George A.) 1965
McMahon, Mary Margaret (John E.) 1985
McMillan, Ann (Douglas D.) 1994
McMillan, Jean Carnes (Malcolm) 1985
  Rowland, Jean (John C.)
  Engle, Jean (Donald)
McNeely, Marjorie (Donald G.) 1954
McNeely, Susan (Harry III) 1998
Mears, Hella (Norman) 1975
  Hueg, Hella (William F., Jr.)
Meek, Sarah (Eric F. Swanson) 2008

Menk, Jane (Louis W.) 1973
Messing, Miriam (Richard F.) 1970
Millard, Jo (Glen E.) 1959
Mills, Arline Griggs (George P.) 1954
Moles, Clotilde Irvine (Edwin J., Jr.) 1956
Moores, Susan (Mark) 2003
Morgan, Annetta D. (John E. P.) 1952
Moriarty, Edna Cammack (Lester J.) 1965
Mueller, Nancy (Terry) 2012
Mullery, Jane (Charles W.) 1970
Murphy, Judy (John M.) 1982
Murphy, Madeline (Frank) 1952
Musser, Betty (John M.) 1941
Myers, Betty (John H.) 1973
Neset, Karen (David Estreen) 2009
Nicholson, Barbara (David) 1996
Nicholson, Catherine Thayer (Ford J.) 1990
Nuffort, Pam (Robert) 2000
Ober, Agnes (Edgar B.) 1935
Oehler, Betty (Cole) 1977
Oehler, Susan (Jon Seltzer) 2011
Ohmans, Patricia (Tony Schmitz) 2013
Ommen, Jerilynn (Gordon) 2011
Oppenheimer, Christine (James R.) 1970
Ordway, Charlotte Partridge (John Gilman) 1931
Ordway, Jessie Gilman (Lucius Pond) 1928
Ordway, Margaret/Marge (John G., Jr.) 1957
Ordway, Marla (John G. III) 1993
Ordway, Gladys Ford (Richard) 1931
Ozzello, Kimberly (Brian) 2009
Parenteau, Rita (William) 2013
Parker, Gay B. 1985
Peyton, Julia (John N.) 1949
Power, Ginny (Richard K.) 1971
Prampoline Katherine Gillette (Alberto) 1931
Price, Glenna (Milton D., Jr.) 1970
Prokosch, Sharon (Richard) 2003
Pulver, Shannon Murphy (John W.) 1971
Rasmussen, Janelle (Erik) 2012

Ray, Bernice S. (Philip L.) 1953
Reid, Dorothy (Edward S.) 1983
Richards, Virginia Schuneman (E.T. Fraser) 1931
Ridder, Agnes (B.H., Sr.) 1946
Ridder, Jane (Bernard H., Jr.) 1961
Ridder, Cathleen (Peter B.) 1993
Ridder, Kathleen (Robert B.) 1954
Ross, Sally (Hamilton) 1981
Sanborn, Dorothy Cammack (Theodore) 1971
Saunders, Mary Proal (Edward Nelson, Jr.) 1928
Savage, Betty (Thomas C.) 1945
Schatz, Lou (James E.) 1999
Scherer, Nancy (Ken Collier) 2009
Schuneman, Louise Nelson (Albert Lesley) 1931
Schurmeier, Margaret G. (Mrs. G.B.) 1931
Seltzer, Susan (Jon) 2011
Senkler, Pam (Robert) 2000
Shepard, Nancy (Blake) 1975
Shepard, Katherine K. (Roger B.) 1928
Shepard, Rosie (Peter H.) 1983
Shepard, Ruth H. (S. MacMillan, Jr.) 1956
Shields, Helen (Lytton J.) 1935
Slade, Elizabeth/Betty (G. Norman) 1946
Soholt, Paula (Jeffrey) 1998
Stanley, Mary (Richard W.) 1986
Steiner, Lynn (Ted) 2012
Stevenson, Heidi (Robert J.) 1981
St. John, Susan Colby/SuSu 1978
Stott, Gretchen Richter (Charles W.) 1931
Stutz, Tracy (Todd) 2006
Sundberg, Carol (Alfred R., Jr.) 1979
Svendsen, Deni (Arnulf L.) 1989
Sweney, Mary G. (W. Homer) 1952
Sweney, Betty (W.Homer, Jr.) 1961
Talen, Rosalie (James M.) 1985
Taylor, Helen (Orley R.) 1967
Tesar, Elise (George H.) 1991
Thiele, Marian (Stanley W.) 1978
Thompson. Dorothy 1931

Thompson, Geraldine Schurmeier (Horace) 1928
Tiffany, Elizabeth/Betty (Francis B.) 1981
Tiffany, Carol (Francis B.) 1967
Titcomb, Cecie (E. Rodman) 1994
Titcomb, Julie (Edward R.) 1965
Turner, Roddie 1994
Umhoefer, Christine (David B.) 2006
Valleau, Gerry (R. Thomas) 1966
Venker, Deb (Mike) 2009
Wahlstrom, JoAnne (John) 2009
Ward, Jane (F. John) 1954
Ward, Mary (William E.) 1940
Washburn, Adelaide (Harold O.) 1949
Weed, Alice (George) 1958
Weyerhaeuser, Harriette Davis (F.E.) 1931
Weyerhaeuser, Nancy (F.T.) 1989
Weyerhaeuser, Peggy (Fred) 1954
  Harmon, Peggy (Reuel D.)
Weyerhaeuser, Vivian (F.K.) 1952
Whitaker, Carol (William) 1991
  Kolb, Carol (Ron)
Whitaker, Julie (Charles) 1997
White, Anne Turney (Edwin) 1931
Williams, Gloria/G.G. (Richard) 2012
Wilsey, Shari Taylor (Roger D., Sr.) 2000/2009
Winship, Karen B. 1994
Winter, Karen (Norbert F.) 1985
Wright, Margaret Ames (Cushing F.) 1931
Zechmann, Susan/Sue (James) 2001
Zelle, Ann (Louis N.) 1975

*Founding members in bold type

155

Illustration Credits

Most of the photographs in this book have been donated to the Saint Paul Garden Club Archives by club members. We are very grateful to the club's historians, Geraldine Thompson, Miriam Messing, Ruth Shepard, Barbara Bentson, Joan Duddingston, Lee Driscoll, and Deni Svendsen for their archival work; and, particularly, to Julie Titcomb for carefully preserving the club's early photographs. We offer our hearty thanks to them, as well as to the many individuals and organizations listed below who gave us permission to publish their photographs.

Pages 27-30. Photos courtesy of Minnesota State Horticultural Society.

Page 31. Photo courtesy of Children's Hospitals and Clinics of Minnesota.

Page 32. Photo courtesy of Leonard Gloeb. Photo of arbors courtesy of JoAnne Wahlstrom.

Page 35. Photo courtesy of the Victory Garden Foundation.

Page 36. Photo courtesy of Hennepin County Library Special Collections.

Page 37. Photo courtesy of Community Design Center (now Urban Roots).

Page 62. Photo courtesy of Joanne Wahlstrom.

Pages 77, 78. Photos courtesy of Colles and John Larkin.

Page 81. Photos by Sarah Crandall, courtesy of Angel Crandall.

Pages 84, 86, 87, 118. Photos courtesy of Dodge Nature Center.

Page 104. Photo courtesy of Susan Brust.

Page 109. Photo courtesy of Somerset Elementary School.

Page 110. Photo courtesy of Expo Elementary School.

Page 111. Photo courtesy of Eco Education.